Selected Works of Frits Albers Volume 2

Vatican II

Defense of the Novus Ordo Missae

Five Smooth Stones (1 Sam. 17:40) – On Modern Trends and How to Deal with Them

Frits Albers

Edited by Frank Calneggia

⊕ENROUTE
Make the time

En Route Books and Media, LLC
5705 Rhodes Avenue
St. Louis, MO 63109

Cover credit: Sebastian Mahfood from the Miraculous Crucifix of San Marcello in the Church of San Marcello al Corso, in Rome, Italy

ISBN-13: 979-8-88870-194-2
Library of Congress Control Number:
Available at https://catalog.loc.gov

Dedication

Dedicated, with great respect to the memory of Pope Paul VI, who literally lived Vatican II in the embrace of all who came to visit him, and who taught Vatican II in his everlasting encyclicals.

On the Feast of the Holy Rosary
October 7th, 1978

Quotations

#5 ....for the presentation of the Gospel message is not an optional contribution for the Church. It is the duty incumbent on her by the command of the Lord Jesus, so that people can believe and be saved. This message is indeed necessary. It is unique. It cannot be replaced. It does not permit either indifference, syncretism or accommodation. It is a question of people's salvation. It is the beauty of the Revelation that it represents. It brings with it a wisdom that is not of this world. It is able to stir up by itself faith - faith that rests on the power of God.[11] It is truth. It merits having the apostle consecrate to it all his time and all his energies, and to sacrifice for it, if necessary, his own life. [11] Cf. 1 *Cor* 2:5.

#9 As the kernel and center of His Good News, Christ proclaims salvation, this great gift of God which is liberation from everything that oppresses man but which is above all liberation from sin and the Evil One, in the joy of knowing God and being known by Him, of seeing Him, and of being given over to Him. All of this is begun during the life of Christ and definitively accomplished by His death and resurrection. But it must be patiently carried on during the course of history, in order to be realized fully on the day of the final coming of Christ, whose date is known to no one except the Father.

#14 Evangelizing is in fact the grace and vocation proper to the Church, her deepest identity. She exists in order to evangelize, that is to say, in order to preach and teach, to be the channel of the gift of grace, to reconcile sinners with God, and to perpetuate Christ's sacrifice in the Mass, which is the memorial of His death and glorious resurrection.

Pope St. Paul VI, Apostolic Exhortation
Evangelii Nuntiandi, Dec 8, 1975

#2. From the beginning of my pastoral ministry in the See of Peter, I have taken care to "state the lasting importance of the Second Vatican Council" calling attention to "our clear duty to devote our energies to putting it into effect". Our efforts have been directed towards "bringing to maturity in the sense of movement and of life the fruitful seeds which the Fathers of the Ecumenical Council, nourished by the word of God, cast upon the good soil (cf Mt 13:8, 23), that is, their authoritative teaching and pastoral decisions" (3). On several occasions I have developed various aspects of the conciliar teaching on the Liturgy (4) and have emphasized the importance of the Constitution *Sacrosanctum Concilium* for the life of the people of God: in it "the substance of that ecclesiological doctrine which would later be put before the conciliar Assembly is already evident. The Constitution *Sacrosanctum Concilium*, the first conciliar document, anticipated" (5) the Dogmatic Constitution *Lumen Gentium* on the Church and amplified, in its turn, the teaching of the Constitution. After a quarter of a century, during which both the Church and society have experienced profound and rapid changes, it is a fitting moment to throw light on the importance of the Conciliar Constitution, its relevance in relation to new problems and the enduring value of its principles.

#3. In response to the requests of the Fathers of the Council of Trent, concerned with the reform of the Church in their time, Pope Saint Pius V saw to the reform of the liturgical books, above all the Breviary and the Missal. It was towards this same goal that succeeding Roman Pontiffs directed their energies during the subsequent centuries in order to ensure that the rites and liturgical books were brought up to date and when necessary clarified. From the beginning of this century they undertook a more general reform. Pope Saint Pius X established a special Commission for this reform and he thought that it would take a number of years for it to complete its work; however he laid the foundation stone of this edifice by renewing the Roman Breviary. (6) "In fact this all demands" he affirmed, "according to the views of the experts, a work both detailed and extensive; and therefore it is necessary that many years should pass, before this liturgical edifice, so to speak,…reappears in new splendour in its dignity and harmony, once the marks of old age have been cleared away" (7).

Pope Pius XII took up again the great project of liturgical reform by issuing the Encyclical Mediator Dei (8) and by establishing a new Commission. (9) He likewise decided important matters for example: authorizing a new version of the Psalter to facilitate the understanding of the Psalms; (10) the modification of the Eucharistic fast in order to facilitate access to Holy Communion; the use of contemporary language in the Ritual; and, above all, the reform of the Easter Vigil (11) and Holy Week (12). The introduction to the Roman Missal of 1963 was preceded by the declaration of Pope John XXIII, according to which "the fundamental principles, related to the general reform of the Liturgy, were to be entrusted to the Fathers in the forthcoming Ecumenical Council". (13)

#4. Such an overall reform of the Liturgy was in harmony with the general hope of the whole Church. In fact, the liturgical spirit had become more and more widespread together with the desire for an "active participation in the most holy mysteries and in the public and solemn prayer of the Church", (14) and a wish to hear the word of God in more abundant measure. Together with the biblical renewal, the ecumenical movement, the missionary impetus and ecclesiological research, the reform of the Liturgy was to contribute to the overall renewal of the Church. I draw attention to this in the Letter *Dominicae Cenae*: "A very close and organic bond exists between the renewal of the Liturgy and the renewal of the whole life of the Church. The Church not only acts but also expresses herself in the Liturgy and draws from the Liturgy the strength for her life". (15).

The reform of the rites and the liturgical books was undertaken immediately after the promulgation of the Constitution *Sacrosanctum Concilium* and was brought to an effective conclusion in a few years thanks to the considerable and selfless work of a large number of experts and bishops from all parts of the world (16).

This work was undertaken in accordance with the conciliar principles of fidelity to tradition and openness to legitimate development (17); and so it is possible to say that the reform of the Liturgy is strictly traditional and in accordance with "the ancient usage of the holy Fathers". (18).

#6. .... Since Christ's Death on the Cross and his Resurrection constitute the content of the daily life of the Church (25) and the pledge of his eternal Passover, (26) the Liturgy has as its first task to lead us untiringly back to the Easter pilgrimage initiated by Christ, in which we accept death in order to enter into life.

#9. .... The Church manifests herself as one, with that unity which comes to her from the Trinity, (37) especially when the holy people of God participates "in the one Eucharist, in one and the same prayer, at the one altar, presided over by the bishop surrounded by his presbyterate and his ministers". (38) Let nothing in the celebration of the Liturgy disrupt or obscure this unity of the Church!

.... In liturgical celebration the Church expresses her catholicity, since in her the Spirit of the Lord gathers together people of all languages in the profession of the same faith (42) and from East to West presents to God the Father the offering of Christ, and offers herself together with him. (43)

.... In the Liturgy the Church manifests herself as apostolic, because the faith that she professes is founded upon the witness of the apostles; because in the celebration of the mysteries, presided over by the bishop, successor of the apostle, or by a minister ordained in the apostolic succession, she faithfully hands on what she has received from the Apostolic Tradition; and because the worship which she renders to God commits her to the mission of spreading the Gospel in the world.

#11. ... It can also be supposed that the transition from simply being present, very often in a rather passive and silent way, to a fuller and more active participation has been for some people too demanding. Different and even contradictory reactions to the reform have resulted from this. Some have received the new books with a certain indifference, or without trying to understand the reasons for the changes; others, unfortunately, have turned back in a one-sided and exclusive way to the previous liturgical forms which some of them consider to be the sole guarantee of certainty in faith. Others have promoted outlandish innovations, departing from the norms issued by the authority of the Apostolic See or the bishops, thus disrupting the unity of the Church and the piety of the faithful and even on occasion contradicting matters of faith.

#14. The Constitution *Sacrosanctum Concilium* is the expression of the unanimous voice of the College of Bishops gathered around the Successor of Peter and with the help of the Spirit of Truth promised by the Lord Jesus (cf. Jn 15:26). The Constitution continues to sustain the Church along the paths of renewal and of holiness by fostering genuine liturgical life.

The principles enunciated in that document are an orientation also for the future of the Liturgy, in such a way that the liturgical reform may be ever better understood and implemented. "It is therefore necessary and urgent to actuate a new and *intensive education* in order to discover all the riches contained in the Liturgy. (65)

#15. The most urgent task is that of the biblical and liturgical formation of the people of God, both pastors and faithful. The Constitution had already stressed this: "There is no hope that this may come to pass unless pastors of souls themselves become imbued more deeply with the spirit and power of the liturgy so as to become masters of it". (64) This is a long-term programme, which must begin in the seminaries and houses of formation (65) and continue throughout their priestly life. (66) A formation suited to their state is indispensable also for lay people, (67) especially since in many regions they are called upon to assume ever more important responsibilities in the community.

#16. Another important task for the future is that of the adaptation of the Liturgy to different cultures. The Constitution set forth the principle, indicating the procedure to be followed by the bishops' conferences. (68) ... There remains the considerable task of continuing to implant the Liturgy in certain cultures, welcoming from them those expressions which are compatible with aspects of the *true and authentic spirit of the Liturgy*, in respect for the *substantial unity of the Roman Rite* as expressed in the liturgical books. (69) The adaptation must take account of the fact that in the Liturgy, and notably that of the sacraments, there is a *part which is unchangeable*, because it is of divine institution, and of which the Church is the guardian. There are also *parts open to change*, which the Church has the power and on occasion also the duty to adapt to the cultures of recently evangelized peoples. (70) This is not a new problem for the Church." (71)

#23. The time has come to renew that spirit which inspired the Church at the moment when the Constitution *Sacrosanctum Concilium* was prepared, discussed, voted upon and promulgated, and when the first steps were taken to apply it. The seed was sown; it has known the rigours of winter, but the seed has sprouted, and become a tree. It is a matter of the organic growth of a tree becoming ever stronger the deeper it sinks its roots into the soil of tradition. (95)

Pope St. John Paul II

Apostolic Letter *Vicesimus Quintus Annus*
On the 25th Anniversary of the Promulgation of the Conciliar
Constitution "Sacrosanctum Concilium"
On the Sacred Liturgy, Dec 4, 1988

#675 Before Christ's second coming the Church must pass through a final trial that will shake the faith of many believers. The persecution that accompanies her pilgrimage on earth will unveil the 'mystery of iniquity' in the form of a religious deception offering men an apparent solution to their problems at the price of apostasy from the truth. The supreme religious deception is that of the Antichrist, a pseudo-messianism by which man glorifies himself in place of God and of his Messiah come in the flesh."

#676 The Antichrist's deception already begins to take shape in the world every time the claim is made to realize within history that messianic hope which can only be realized beyond history through the eschatological judgement. The Church has rejected even modified forms of this falsification of the kingdom to come under the name of millenarianism, especially the 'intrinsically perverse' political form of a secular messianism.

#677 The Church will enter the glory of the kingdom only through this final Passover, when she will follow the Lord in his death and resurrection. The kingdom will be fulfilled, then, not by a historic triumph of the Church through a progressive ascendancy, but only by God's victory over the final unleashing of evil, which will cause his Bride to come down from heaven. God's triumph over the revolt of evil will take the form of the Last Judgment after the final cosmic upheaval of this passing world.

Catechism of the Catholic Church.

We find ourselves in the presence of the greatest confrontation in history, the greatest mankind had ever to confront. We are facing the final confrontation between the Church and the Anti-Church, between the Gospel and the Anti-Gospel.

Cardinal Karol Wojtyla
Cracow, Poland. June 24, 1977

You saw Hell where the souls of poor sinners go. In order to save them, God wishes to establish in the world devotion to my Immaculate Heart. If people do what I ask, many souls will be saved and there will be peace. The war is going to end. But if people do not stop offending God, another, even worse war, will begin in the reign of Pius XI. When you see a night illumined by an unknown light, know that it is the great sign that God gives you that He is going to punish the world by means of war, hunger and persecution of the Church and of the Holy Father. To prevent it I shall come to ask for the Communion of reparation on the first Saturdays. If people heed my requests, Russia will be converted and the world will have peace. If not, Russia will spread its errors throughout the world, fomenting wars and persecutions of the Church.

The good will be martyred, the Holy Father will have much to suffer, and various nations will be annihilated. In the end my Immaculate Heart will triumph. The Holy Father will consecrate Russia to me and it will be converted. A period of peace will be granted
to the world. In Portugal the dogmas of the Faith will always be
kept. (Here follows the third secret, revealed by Pope John Paul II
in 2000).

Our Lady of Fatima, July 13, 1917

But you are a chosen race, a royal priesthood, a holy nation,
God's own people, that you may declare the wonderful deeds of
him who called you out of darkness into his marvelous light.

1 Peter 2:9

#723 Today I heard these words: .... "I perform works of mercy
in every soul. The greater the sinner, the greater the right he has to
My mercy. My mercy is confirmed in every work of My hands. He
who trusts in My mercy will not perish, for all his affairs are Mine,
and his enemies will be shattered at the base of My footstool".

#1588 Today I heard the words: "In the Old Covenant I sent
prophets wielding thunderbolts to My people. Today I am sending
you with My mercy to the people of the whole world. I do not want
to punish aching mankind, but I desire to heal it, pressing it to My
Merciful Heart. I use punishment when they themselves force Me

to do so; My hand is reluctant to take hold of the sword of justice. Before the Day of Justice I am sending the Day of Mercy".

Diary of Saint Maria Faustina Kowalska

After the two parts which I have already explained, at the left of Our Lady and a little above, we saw an Angel with a flaming sword in his left hand; flashing, it gave out flames that looked as though they would set the world on fire; but they died out in contact with the splendour that Our Lady radiated towards him from her right hand: pointing to the earth with his right hand, the Angel cried out in a loud voice: "Penance, Penance, Penance!". And we saw in an immense light that is God: "something similar to how people appear in a mirror when they pass in front of it" a Bishop dressed in White "we had the impression that it was the Holy Father". Other Bishops, Priests, men and women Religious going up a steep mountain, at the top of which there was a big Cross of rough-hewn trunks as of a cork-tree with the bark; before reaching there the Holy Father passed through a big city half in ruins and half trembling with halting step, afflicted with pain and sorrow, he prayed for the souls of the corpses he met on his way; having reached the top of the mountain, on his knees at the foot of the big Cross he was killed by a group of soldiers who fired bullets and arrows at him, and in the same way there died one after another the other Bishops, Priests, men and women Religious, and various lay people of different ranks and positions. Beneath the two arms of the Cross there were two Angels each with a crystal aspersorium in his hand, in which they gathered up the blood of the Martyrs and with it sprinkled the souls that were making their way to God.

The third part of the secret revealed at the Cova da Iria-Fatima, on 13 July 1917.

I write in obedience to you, my God, who command me to do so through his Excellency the Bishop of Leiria and through your Most Holy Mother and mine. Sister Lucia dos Santos Tuy-3-1-1944.

Pope Saint John Paul II. April 19, 2000

Table of Contents

Foreword

Following the publication of *Selected Works of Frits Albers Vol 1: Analysing The Errors And Exposing The Real Agenda Of Pierre Teilhard de Chardin S.J.*, we have decided to publish a second volume of his works.

Selected for publication in this second volume of the works of Frits Albers are the following three written in the 1970s.

Vatican II;

In Defense of the Novus Ordo Missae of His Holiness Pope Paul VI;

Five Smooth Stones

A principal reason for publishing anew these books written almost fifty years ago can be gathered from the author's own words taken from his *Vatican II.*

"It is from our era, and from the Church of our era, still so close to us, that we must wrestle to partly unlock the mystique contained in the very essence of Vatican II. For our own immediate benefit as well as for the benefit of the Catholics to whom Catholic Tradition must be handed over in its entirety. No doubt Vatican II has a clear message for the Church of the future, but this great Council happened *in our time*, and future generations of Catholics depend on us - on how well we understood that time. How well our Catholic children will comprehend the *past* which happens to be our *present*, depends entirely on us."

Many of the Catholic children of that era (and now their children also) hold positions of responsibility in society and in the Church. The younger generations of Catholics who were born after

Vatican II and the promulgation of the Novus Ordo, if they take to heart the author's words quoted above, should derive no little profit from the works presented in this volume. That brings us to the first of these three works, *Vatican II*.

In the first chapter the author surveys the pre-Vatican II Catholic scene and identifies two broad groups of Catholics. The first group consists of those who tried to live within the Tradition of the Church as they knew and understood it. The second group consists of those who had abandoned that Tradition and replaced it with a new and foreign 'outlook' on Catholicism of which Communism would be one logical expression.

In the second chapter the author brings forth evidence to show that the Catholic Faith of the first group passed through its conciliar examination with its orthodoxy confirmed and was acknowledged as essentially good, even if in need of some correction concerning the way the Faith was put into practise. He then shows that the 'New Catholicism' of the second group, when presented at the Council, was sifted out and rejected. He quotes substantially from the documents of Vatican II to prove his arguments and to show that the Council can only be rightly understood when seen as a continuation of the uninterrupted Tradition that goes back to the Apostles.

The third chapter deals with the way errors and heresies rejected by the Council were forced into the Church immediately after the Council by means of a bypass around the Council. Modernism, the source of these collective errors and heresies, particularly the systematic modernism of Teilhard de Chardin; false ecumenism, communism and socialism had all been condemned by Popes long before Vatican II and are therefore outside the Living Tradition of the Church. Consequently, these errors and heresies can neither be traced to nor identified with the Council and its Voice of Living Catholic Tradition; neither then, nor now, nor in the future.

The fourth chapter deals with rejected 'religious' doctrines and practices found in the bypass discussed in the previous chapter. The author focuses some attention on doctrines and practices which are being used to bring about a global religious unification of the world under evil. This 'religious' phenomena, found in the bypass around Vatican II, and its subservience to global political evil were identified and written about by Pope St Pius X in 1910. Vatican II can be blamed neither for its doctrines nor practices, nor for the 'ecumenical inspiration' to join it.

The fifth and final chapter is devoted to overcoming the 'One World Church' identified by Pope S. Pius X. With the aid of a number of authentic Catholic sources the author provides convincing evidence that Vatican II was meant to prepare the Church for this onslaught of evil and to show Catholics how to put their Faith into practise under such trying conditions. This pastoral initiative and encouragement of the Council, the author holds, is shared in by the reform of the Holy Mass.

That brings us to the second work in this volume, *In Defense of the Novus Ordo Missae of His Holiness Pope Paul VI.*

In this work the author first discusses the 'Una Voce' organisation and the vocations and ordinations of the young men who enter its seminaries. He then goes back to the era when the Latin Mass Associations were first formed in the 1970s.

In his discussion and analysis of the germination of the Latin
Mass Society in Australia (it will be the same in principle elsewhere) he shows beyond doubt that their first argument to vindi-
cate their rejection of the Novus Ordo was based on the wording of
Quo Primum, the Papal Bull by which Pope St. Pius V promulgated
the reform of the Mass called for by the Council of Trent. The
younger generations of Catholics referred to above, the ones who
were born after the promulgation of the Novus Ordo (and who
consequently were meant by the Church to be raised as Catholics
in the Novus Ordo), would do well to take to heart the author's
refutation of this still repeated focal point of indoctrination by
which many have been convinced into going over to the old rite
and into rejecting the Novus Ordo and Vatican II.

The author examines and answers the main arguments of the
Latin Mass Associations in four chapters: (1) Argument From History; (2) Argument From Tradition; (3) Argument From Theology;
(4) Argument From Faith.

The arguments used by the Latin Mass Associations and repeated to this day over "for many" versus "for all"; "use of the vernacular"; "ad orientem" are all evaluated and answered.

To conclude the author assesses the responses of the Priestly
Fraternity of St. Peter to the decisions and directives of the Pontifical Commission *Ecclesia Dei* set up by Pope St. John Paul II to
watch over the doctrines and govern the practises of that Fraternity.

The third and final selection presented in this volume is *Five
Smooth Stones*. It is subtitled "A Paper on Modern Trends and
How to Deal with them". The author discusses five modern trends

- one in each of the five Sections of the work. In each Section he shows Catholics how to deal with the errors and evils being discussed in that Section. The five Sections are named as follows: (1) Moses and the Inerrancy of Scripture as the Word of God; (2) The Mystique of Vatican II and the Unbroken Tradition in the Catholic Church; (3) Fatima and the Discipline of the Mind; (4) The Communion of Saints and Catholic Resourcefulness; (5) Modernists' Meanest Mischief.

May the three works included in this present volume bring instruction, guidance and hope to Catholics in their quest to advance in knowledge and love of holy Mother Church and its life giving Teaching and to dispel the dark clouds of confusion, error and subterfuge they have to deal with in modern day 'catholic' environments, and finally to give them sound practical guidance on how to overcome and defeat the real enemy.

To conclude this Foreword I would like to draw attention to a prayer indulgenced by Pope St. Pius X with the hope that readers will include it daily in their armoury against evil.

"August Queen of Heaven, sovereign Mistress of the Angels, who did receive from the beginning the mission and the power to crush Satan's head, we beseech thee to send thy holy Angels, that under thy command and by thy power, they may pursue the evil spirits, encounter them on every side, resist their bold attacks, and drive them hence into the abyss of woe.

Who is like God! O good and tender Mother you will always be our love and our hope.

Most Holy Mother, send thy Angels to defend us and to drive the cruel enemy from us. Amen.

All you holy Angels and Archangels help and defend us. Amen."

Book I

Vatican II

Frits Albers, Ph.B.

First Edition
On the Feast of the Holy Rosary,
Saturday, October 7th, 1978.

Second Edition
Holy Week, 1995.

Third Edition
February 2, 2000.

Fourth Edition
June 7, 2024

Preface

This third edition of *Vatican II* is a reworked update of an article of mine that was first published on the Feast of the Holy Rosary, Saturday, October 7, 1978, and reprinted in 1995. It is being made available with the same hope that accompanied the first edition: that it may help Catholic readers to understand a bit better the deep Mystery that lies hidden in this great Council of the Holy Church that caused the writing of this little booklet in the first place.

It is by now an open secret that the Second Vatican Council is viewed by many orthodox Catholics, if not with a sort of latent hostility, then at least with open suspicion. This is largely (but, as we will see, not exclusively, for God never removes from us our free will) the direct result of the fury and ferocity with which the Modernists have seized on the post-Conciliar period in their determination to be heard as the exclusive interpreters of the letter and the spirit of this Council. Their relentless drive has created the unavoidable impression that all the modern heresies can be traced back to this great Council. And the silence and timidity of the ones, appointed by God to be the authentic teachers in the Church (with the notable exception of the late Pope Paul VI and some very courageous bishops) did not help much to restore morale and confidence.

When my article *In Defence of the Novus Ordo* did the rounds, the reaction of not a few was "that Vatican II had itself to blame for the run-down of the Liturgy". Others reacted to my latest article *Our Lady* with the incredulous reply: "But Vatican II is supposed to have downgraded devotion to Our Lady ..." They found it hard to believe that so much beautiful teaching on the Mother of God, "the New Eve" and "the Mother of the Church" could come from a Council which had so obviously been subject to much dilution from the 'Rhine': the Northern Alliance of liberal bishops and their so-called 'experts'.

That, under these circumstances, many good Catholics are confused about Vatican II, is understandable. And then it does not help to recommend the teachings of the Second Vatican Council to these good and simple Catholics, if they repeatedly hear from teachers, catechists, Priests and other experts that they are too much pre-Vatican II in their thinking. For this rebuke contains the barb that Vatican II made essential changes in doctrine, and that the old is no longer acceptable.

In support of the above it is possible to quote our present Holy Father from a recent address he gave to a group of North American Bishops at their "Ad Limina" visit on October 9, 1998. In this speech the Holy Father made the following observation:

"To look back over what has been done in the field of liturgical renewal in the years since the Council is, first, to see many reasons for giving heartfelt thanks and praise to the Most Holy Trinity for the marvelous awareness which has developed among the faithful of their role and responsibility in this priestly work of Christ and His Church. It is also to realise that not all changes have always and everywhere been accompanied by the necessary explanation and catechesis. As a result, in some cases there has been a misunderstanding of the very nature of the liturgy, leading to abuses, polarization, and sometimes even grave scandal. After the experience of more than thirty years of liturgical renewal, we are well placed to assess both the strength and the weakness of what has been done, in order more confidently to plot our course into the future which God has in mind for His cherished People".

Adding my humble comments to the above quoted remarks of Pope John Paul II, I would like to repeat what I wrote on Oct. 23, 1977 to a distinguished Roman theologian, in reply to a letter of his to me (May 25):

"To me, it is an article of faith, that it is absolutely impossible and useless to consider and discuss Vatican II without an absolute acceptance, i.e. an acceptance in Faith, of the Eternal Truths taught by the pre-Vatican II Church. The same Church that gave us the *Syllabus of Errors* gave us Vatican II. If I cannot induce my adversary to agree with me on pre-Vatican II teachings, it is utterly futile to look with him at Vatican II. If he attacks me for my adherence to pre-Vatican II teachings, he is bound to disagree with me on the authentic interpretation to be given to the teachings of Vatican II, because this authentic interpretation can only come from an uninterrupted Catholic Tradition. If my articles are rejected because of my adherence to pre-Vatican II sources and teachings, they will be rejected because of my adherence to authentic Vatican II teachings. In fact, we see this plainly happening already: the teilhardians are so disillusioned with Vatican II, that they only casually, almost from reflex, link their erroneous effluent to this great Council. They know by now that their teachings are *not* found there, and they are looking forward to *Vatican III*, or *Jerusalem II*. The Holy Father Pope Paul VI himself is almost exclusively pre-Vatican II lately, linking up the teachings of this Council with Catholic Tradition".

This reference to 'Vatican III' became substantiated with the appearance of the book called *Toward Vatican III* some 7 months later (mid 1978) containing the papers of the same "world famous theologians" and "experts" who, with their declaration in the *London Times* immediately prior to the Conclave, convened for the election of a successor to the late Pontiff Pope Paul VI, demanded stringent reforms of the Papacy, calling on the Cardinals not only to elect "*a worldly pope*", but also, prior to the election, "*to ponder over the Ten Point proposal contained in their joint declaration, and to devote the first part of this month's conclave to a discussion of the declaration before they elected a new Pope*". (Are we not constantly reminded, in dealing with these people, of the immortal words of His Holiness Pope St. Pius X in his encyclical *Pascendi*: "*Audacity is their chief characteristic*"?)

It is instructive to read in the "joint declaration" that the Cardinals are urged by these heretics "*to elect a pope who will not be a doctrinaire defender of ancient bastions ... and who will share power with the bishops...*" And in case the good Cardinals missed the point, the declaration "*suggested the need for a reform of the papacy as an institution, with the pope looking on the synod of bishops as a responsible decision-making body*". Neither the language nor the intentions could be any clearer.

I have read *Toward Vatican III*, and, as is to be expected, it is empty of *Theologia Sacra* and full of human and social engineering, values clarifications, contradictions of Catholic Teaching and even heresies. It is a monumental testimony by the architects of the

"*One-World Church*" of their final rejection of Vatican II. Unable to trace their frightful dissent any longer to this great and mysterious Council, they have resolved to make it the blue-print of a future 'council', so that already this dissent can be given the immediate benefit and respectability of "inevitable conciliar teachings" of the future ...

Finally, a word about the well-known book by Fr. Ralph Wiltgen, SVD: *The Rhine Flows into the Tiber*. This book, more than anything else, should explain why the above-mentioned architects of the "*Church of Darkness*" are despairing of Vatican II. The Council simply did not go their way in spite of the apparent dominant influence of the 'Rhine': the Northern Alliance of the liberal-catholic bishops and their *periti*. Here follows a typical passage of the book, p. 158, expressing someone's acute disappointment:

"*Prof. Oscar Cullmann*, a guest of the *Secretariat for Promoting Christian Unity*, gave a lengthy press conference at the end of the Council, in the course of which he said:

'We cannot pass over in silence the disappointment that we experienced at seeing the title of *Mediatrix* given to Mary ... The fact that the text on Mary, after so much discussion as to where it should be placed, should have finally become the concluding chapter of the Schema on the Church - a decision which was in fact intended to weaken Mariology - has in reality made it even stronger, because everything stated about the Church culminates, so to speak, in this chapter ... Mariology at this Council has in general been intensified to a degree which is not in keeping with the ecumenical tendencies of Protestantism ... What was expected was a

weakening of emphasis, **not some sort of revision of the fundamental relationship to the Virgin Mary'.**"

Is any further proof needed to show how skilfully the Holy Spirit used the bad intentions of some bishops, even of a dominant
group of bishops, for His own designs? Whoever rejects or even
mistrusts Vatican II on the basis of appearances, like the title of Fr.
Wiltgen's book, should seriously examine their Faith in pre-
Conciliar teachings to see how 'accommodating' this Faith has become to unconsciously held private opinions and prejudices, and
how adept we all had become in cushioning ourselves against the
more uncomfortable demands of the Cross made upon this Faith.

The all-time greatness and mystery of Vatican Council II lies
hidden in the Mystery of the Church and points to the fact that, as
a Beacon in the blackness of 20th century humanity, it has made all
Catholics uncomfortable by the stark outline of a Cross. Not a
Cross safely separated from us by some 2000 years of history, but
the harsh outline of a Cross we have been at pains to overlook, but
which we are now forced to recognize inescapably, as our very
own. Now that many a support we had so earnestly labelled as "essential" simply because we found them so comfortable and reassuring, have been taken away from us, we are suddenly faced with the
duty to measure our pre-Vatican II Faith and the strength it has to
support us in the post-Conciliar turmoil. Or to stay within the parable of Our Lord Himself, *we are faced with the responsibility of
measuring the amount of oil we had taken with us before we fell
asleep ...*

With these thoughts we have strayed from the province of the
Preface (which is to supply a reason *why* the article should be writ-

ten) into the domain of the Introduction, in which is outlined in what light the article should be viewed.

read into the d realit ... the Introduction on ...
print light to be d ... hould be slowed

Introduction

Here I can be brief. I will view the subject-matter of this article in the same Light as I viewed all the others: the Supernatural Light of Divine and Catholic Faith and that of the teachings of the Holy Catholic Church. I do not merely write theology: I write to strengthen the Catholic Faith of my readers: their Faith in that Supernatural Reality here on earth: the Catholic Church.

In earlier articles I examined before them the strange doctrines that have found their way *"into the heart and veins of the Church"* (*Pascendi*), and traced them to their common origin: Teilhard de Chardin and his brand of evolution which is nothing but *systematic Modernism*. At the same time I drew attention to the concerted and global attempts to trace these spurious teachings and principles to the Second Vatican Council, to make them more readily acceptable as genuine, post-Conciliar 'Catholic' insights. This was the necessary spade work for subsequent articles.

In the more recent ones, I have contrasted these twistings of Catholic Dogma with the teachings of the authentic Catholic Magisterium, endeavouring - as already mentioned in the Preface - to show that no authentic pre-Conciliar teaching of the Church can be, nor ever was, at variance with the true teachings of Vatican II. Yet more is required. Vatican II is more than a sum-total of teachings. It has an inspiration all on its own: a uniqueness and mystery which can only be fully resolved in time, when future generations will give glory to God for His loving Providence.

There is something that only *we* can do, for our own generation as well as for the future. *We know* from what Church and from what era this Sacred Council sprung forth, and from where it took root and formation. <u>And this vital information will diminish in time for future generations</u>. In support of this fading of understanding historical values already in the present generation of the young people we may quote the present Holy Father from the same address quoted above to the North American Bishops in Rome when he said:

"... In this sense the young are summoning the whole Church to take the next step in implementing the vision of worship which the Council has bequeathed on us. <u>Unencumbered by the ideological agenda of an earlier time</u> they are able to speak simply and directly of their desire to experience God ...."

The Holy Father is aware that it is a good thing not to be burdened by past ideological strife. But the whole tone of his address is to rectify a wide-spread misconception: that Vatican II constituted a break in Catholic Tradition at least as far as the liturgy of the Church is concerned. For that very reason he was at pains to link the past with the present, going in his address as far back in time as the Fathers and Doctors of the Church.

It is from our era, and from the Church of our era, still so close to us, that we must wrestle to partly unlock the mystique contained in the very essence of Vatican II. For our own immediate benefit as well as for the benefit of the Catholics to whom Catholic Tradition must be handed over in its entirety. No doubt Vatican II has a clear message for the Church of the future, but this great Council happened *in our time*, and future generations of Catholics depend on us how well we understood that time. How well our Catholic children will comprehend the *past* which happens to be our *present*, depends entirely on us.

Chapter One

The Pre-Vatican II Catholic Scene

Broadly speaking, this scene comprises - amongst a multitude of others - two groups of people.

I. Firstly, those who attempt to live entirely within the Tradition of the Roman Catholic Church. Those who take the Church's living Tradition and the teaching of the Magisterium for their rich soil, from which they draw up the sustenance to carry out the command given by the Lord: 'To live in the world but not from the world'. With their sinfulness and their human weaknesses and imperfections, we must still refer to this group as 'the holy people of God'.

Those struggling fathers and mothers who during the years of the Great Depression refused to limit their families by artificial contraception; who reared their children in "the fear of God which is the beginning of Wisdom"; who understood the true meaning of the Church's Sacramental Life and who accepted the necessity for bringing sacrifices themselves in order to partake in this Life. Devotion to the Sacred Heart, to the Mother of God, to the Angels and Saints, Benediction, the Rosary, the giving of alms in support of missionaries in distant countries: all of these found their proper place in a busy life, in which the natural and the Supernatural were never confused but were given their due in a healthy balance. They put great trust and faith in those God had placed over them for the care of their souls and the education of their children: the Bishops, Priests, the good Nuns and Brothers. These in turn came to accept the unquestioning attitude of the good laypeople, and generally speaking were worthy of the trust placed in them.

Although maybe not an idyllic state as anything we become used to tends to 'cushion' us against crosses we do not particularly like and to resistance to changes the Holy Spirit may deem necessary for the salvation of the world - imperfections which the fine filter of Vatican II nevertheless picked up - it was the nearest thing to 'living the Faith' that the Church could expect under the circumstances. Although imperfect, we must realize and acknowledge - in the face of the subsequent monstrous derision from the teilhardians - that it was essentially good, and acknowledged as such by the Council.

Clearly wearied by 400 years of strife with Protestantism, this part of the Catholic scene prior to the Council could be summed up by the motto of the English weekly edition of the *Osservatore Romano*: "*UNICUIQUE SUUM*", "To Each his Due" (or, in effect, "To Each his Own", which is not the same), whilst it unconsciously accepted the safety and reassurance expressed in the second part of the same motto: "*NON PRAEVALEBUNT*": "They will not hold out (against us)" ... But such an obvious sigh for 'peaceful coexistence' (or 'to be left alone') in both the spiritual and temporal order does not make for great apostles to carry out the command of the Lord "to make disciples of all the nations". But then we must not forget that a Saint of that time, the Great Little Flower, *St. Teresa of Lisieux*, did not go out into the whole world either, yet without setting foot outside France, she became the Patron Saint of the Missions.

And so we must assume that many Catholics of this era must have done what she had done in heroic fashion: to sacrifice their daily duty for the Kingdom of God, which means that their lives still became the necessary leaven for the salvation of the world, which, as already remarked earlier, made their life-style essentially good.

This camp was not without its intellectual leaders and thinkers: philosophers, writers, theologians, seminary professors who, faithfully adhering to the anti-modernistic oath, defended the Church's teachings against modernism as they understood it. For, in the long run, only those at the very pinnacle of the Church's intelligentsia remained on guard both against modernism <u>and</u> against evolution: *Jacques Maritain*, Cardinals *Journet* and *Ottaviani*, the great *Jean Danielou*, S.J., philosophers *Dietrich von Hildebrand*, Prof. *Richard Weaver* of Chicago, *Dr. Woodbury* in Australia, and the Dutch Scripture scholar, Prof. Magister. *Dr. J.P.M. van der Ploeg.* But many others, although opposed to Modernism, did not understand the Church's repeated warnings against Teilhardism, and so they ignored them. Thus it came about that through *teilhardian* evolution, Modernism became introduced within the Catholic fold in a *systematic* way.

If we were asked to supply the 'trade mark' by which this group, both the grassroots faithful and their intellectual leaders can be instantly recognized, we would have to point to their belief in the *Real Distinction* between God and His creation, between the Supernatural and the natural, and - what amounts to the same - to their belief in *Absolutes:* Absolute Truth, and an Absolute and Universal Moral Order. For such is the Tradition of the Catholic Church.

Not surprisingly, this Faith went straight through Vatican II, unchanged and unchallenged.

II. And what about their brothers at the other end of the great spectrum of which the pre-Conciliar Church was composed? Here, I must hand you over to that active, restless manipulator and shrewd observer of the world scene for the better part of 40 years: *Whittaker Chambers*, who had this to say in 1964 after his conversion from Communism:

"I am baffled by the way people still speak of the West as if it were at least a cultural unity against Communism. But the West is divided, not only politically, but by an invisible cleavage. On one side are the voiceless masses with their own subdivisions and fractures. On the other side is the enlightened, articulate elite, which to one degree or other has rejected the religious roots of the civilization - the roots without which it is no longer Western Civilization, but a new order of beliefs, attitudes and mandates. In short, this is the order of which Communism is one logical expression. Not originating in Russia, but in the cultural capitals of the West, reaching Russia by clandestine delivery via the old underground centres in Cracow, Vienna, Berne, Zurich and Geneva (WCC). It is a *Western* body of beliefs that now threatens the West from Russia. As a body of Western beliefs, secular, materialistic, rationalistic, the intelligentsia of the West share it, and are therefore always committed to a secret, emotional complicity with Communism" (*Cold Friday*, p. 225-6).

What is stated here so clearly is so serious, that it warrants the most careful attention, to see if it can be corroborated from other sources and evidence. In the following brief but critical analysis I will assume, that a sizeable proportion of the pre-Vatican II elite referred to here, is composed of Catholics.

Now, the above quoted words of Whittaker Chambers can be approached in a variety of ways, but from whichever angle they are studied for their meaning, the conclusion arrived at is always the same.

1. "... elite ...which has rejected the religious roots of the civilization ..."

Catholics belonging to this elite have thus broken away from the first group mentioned in this chapter: the ones who are rooted in the tradition of the Church, drawing sustenance from it for their material and spiritual survival. The spiritual roots of the Western Civilization are not only 'Christian' but Catholic. Rejecting one's spiritual roots therefore, is tantamount to saying that one is looking for, or has already adopted, a new 'Catholic' inspiration.

The hall-mark of the first-mentioned group by which it could be distinctly recognized was its belief in the Supernatural Order as a distinct entity, and by its belief in Absolute Truth and a universal Moral Order. This duality of belief in the Two Cities, the Two Kingdoms, carrying with it the dual obligation of rendering unto Caesar and unto God, and the Real Distinction between them, is part of God's Revelation to Man, is part of the Deposit of Faith of the Church and has been part of the Church's Tradition since Apostolic times.

If all this is rejected by the "elite which pulled up its religious roots from the Civilization", then this vast group must also have adopted a new 'philosophy' which rejects this real distinction between the natural and the Supernatural, allowing utter confusion between the Kingdom of God and the kingdom of this world, truly once again a perfect example of that teilhardian hybrid: *a philosophy of sameness and identity* ....

2. "this is the (new) order of which Communism is one logical expression."

Whoever read the papal encyclical *Divini Redemptoris* of 1937 (remember, we are dealing here with a pre-Vatican II society) knows what His Holiness Pope Pius XI had to say about "*this satanic scourge*": atheistic communism. In this encyclical, the Holy Father did not mince any words:

"This Apostolic See, above all has not refrained from raising its voice, for it knows that its proper and special mission is to defend truth, justice and all those eternal values which Communism ignores or attacks. Ever since the days when groups of intellectuals were formed (Whittaker's *elite*) in an arrogant attempt to free civilization from the bonds of morality and religion, Our Predecessors overtly and explicitly drew the attention of the world to the consequences of the *de-Christianization* of human society. With reference to Communism, Our Ven. Predecessor, Pius IX, of holy memory, as early as 1846 pronounced a solemn condemnation, which he confirmed in the words of the Syllabus directed against *that infamous doctrine of so-called Communism which is absolutely contrary to the Natural Law itself,* and if once adopted would utterly destroy the rights, property and possessions of all men, and even society itself" (#4).

From this teaching it is clear that, if Whittaker's 'Western elite', which pulled up its 'religious roots', has adopted something of 'which Communism would be a logical expression' then this 'new order' they adopted must of necessity, to quote the Holy Father, "be absolutely contrary to the Natural Law itself." Let us see if the Pope can specify this for us.

"According to the doctrine of modern Communism, there is in the world but *one* reality: matter, the *blind* forces of which *evolve* into plant, animal, man. Even human society is nothing but a phenomenon and form of matter, evolving in the same way. In such a doctrine - as is evident - there is no room for the idea of God; there is no difference between matter and spirit, between soul and body; there is neither survival of the soul after death nor any hope in a future life". (#9).

Going by this sacred teaching, Communism rejects the *real distinction* principle, which means that anyone who rejects this principle has then in fact adopted a system, of which Communism would be a logical expression. As we will see in a few moments, there were already innumerable Catholics who even before Vatican II had rejected Thomism and its hated *real distinction* principle.

3. "As a body of Western beliefs: secular, materialistic and rationalistic, the intelligentsia of the West share it and are therefore always committed to a secret, emotional complicity with communism".

Can anyone hope for a more succinct paraphrasing of the papal words than this resume? What did the Western intelligentsia adopt after uprooting itself from its religious past, and which was secular, materialistic and rationalistic to such an extent that Communism was not only a logical expression of this new philosophy, but which also gave the adherents of this new order a great psychological affinity to Communism?

The answer of course is *evolution*, even if the Catholic section of the Western intelligentsia tries to minimize the mental switch by stressing that theirs is *teilhardian* evolution. There is no other contender on the horizon.

Let us pause for a moment and consider what we have achieved so far.

The first group of Catholics is well defined. We know it presented itself into the presence of Vatican II and, with suitable updating, was allowed through. But what about the second group? That they embraced teilhardian evolution, no one, not even they themselves, will deny. And so, for this group, the crucial question was:

"Did they, in embracing teilhardism, uproot themselves from Catholic Tradition, or is teilhardism merely a legitimate interpretation of Catholicism which does not necessitate uprooting oneself from Tradition?"

We may reframe the question in a different way within the framework of the facts discovered so far:

> ➤ "Is it possible to remain in Catholic Tradition and reject the religious roots of one's Catholic civilization?"
> ➤ "Is it possible to remain in Catholic Tradition and espouse a doctrine which is diametrically opposed to it?"
> ➤ "Is it possible to reject the real distinction from a Tradition which is bound up with it, and then to believe that God can create while still evolving Himself with matter and man until 'omega-point' has been reached, as Teilhard postulates?"
> ➤ "Is it possible to remain rooted in Catholic Tradition eternally opposed to atheistic Communism, at the same time

adopting a philosophy from which Communism would be a logical expression?" (It is necessary to remember in this context that it was Pope *Pius XII* who wrote authoritatively in 1950 that "the false evolutionary notions would advance the spread of Communism" (*Humani Generis*), linking the two as with an unbreakable bond. Now the 1962 *Monita* against Teilhard's evolutionary notions have branded them as "false", with the inevitable consequence of advancing Communism and the spread of error.)

➤ Finally, "Is it possible to be steeped in Catholic Tradition, and to embrace a body of Western beliefs: secular, material-istic, rationalistic, which tie the believers not only <u>logically</u> to Communism, but also <u>emotionally</u>, so that, with Com-munism, they become logically <u>and</u> emotionally opposed *"to the very Tradition which condemned Communism?"*

Since the answers to the above questions are obvious, Whittaker Chambers was right, and so were the Popes of the *Syllabus of Errors*, of *Pascendi*, of *Divini Redemptoris*, of *Humani Generis* and of the *Monita* against de Chardin. The teilhardians are no longer in Catholic Tradition, and it will be interesting to see what happened when they presented themselves, individually and as a noisy group, at the gates of Vatican II.

But first, what about the spread of Teilhardism? Was it far enough in 1962 to be taken into consideration?

There is plenty of evidence that the spread of Teilhard de Chardin's ideas is worldwide and that many of the great names in Catholic theology have lent their name and their prestige to the spread of his errors. With the inevitable consequence that they are now dying for a 'church', a 'pope' and a 'council' which will back them up. But history, common sense and Catholic Faith will teach them that it will be a 'church', a 'pope' and a 'council' *outside* Catholic Tradition.

"Whatever reservations one may have about the decision (to make a selection out of the *welter of teilhardian papers available*), we feel nevertheless that the selection presented in this volume has the advantage of bringing out with equal clarity both the theoretical and practical aspects of the author's *theological thought*. In recent years much has been published about *Teilhard de Chardin's* theological writings, both about *his theology* as a whole and about particular points in *his teaching* (see note below).

Seldom in the history of theology has a writer's thought been the occasion in so few years of so much, often passionate, study and discussion. The number and the quality of the studies devoted to his work in this field make it abundantly clear, how insistently Père Teilhard's thought has captured the attention of theologians, and what an unusually powerful stimulus it is to theological speculation of our day.

Apart from Christological questions, most of the essays in this volume deal primarily with the *problem* (sic!) of *Original Sin*. While some of his suggestions may still seem somewhat tentatively expressed, *there can nevertheless be little doubt that it is **in the direction he indicates** that theological research on this issue is being pursued.*"

(*Prof. N. M. Wildiers*, Docteur en Théologie, in a Foreword to a book by Teilhard: *Christianity and Evolution*, French edition, 1969, English translation, Collins 1971).

This frank *Foreword* is remarkable for a number of reasons.

1. There is no indication that there ever was a Vatican Council II. Its existence and findings are totally ignored. Business as usual, even if the business is flagrant Modernism.
2. Teilhard's ideas are seriously called a 'theology'.
3. It is claimed here that his influence is unquestioned.

But Teilhard has rejected the Dogma of Original Sin as formulated and taught by the Tradition of the Church and has rejected the existence of Adam and Eve as a unique first pair. (Both his 1922 and 1947 papers on *Original Sin* are in this volume).

So, if the interest in Teilhard's 'theology' is as worldwide as this man wants us to believe, and if this worldwide interest *and research* is being pursued in the direction of Teilhard's *rejection* of the Dogma of Original Sin, then rejection and contradiction of Dogma is now - for the first time in the history of the Catholic Church - not only graced with the name 'theology', but is being held up as *the* theology of the Catholic Church.

This shows the rejection of the Real Distinction between Good and Evil, between Truth and its contradiction, and the adoption of the principle of *sameness* and identity, by means of which the 'doctrine' is being taught that evil and sin have been abolished so as to become another (and even more acceptable) form of 'good', and that truth *and* its contradiction and denial are equally the same.

This principle is found to lie at the root of any evolutionary 'philosophy' in which everything: god, truth, good, evil, natural, supernatural become reduced to one evolving entity, where sin is explained away as merely being a 'statistical mistake' ...

4. NOTE. "His teachings ...."

In 1926 Teilhard's Superiors forbade him to teach any longer. In 1947, the year of the appearance of his most 'sophisticated' rejection of the Dogma of *Original Sin*, this prohibition to teach was underscored and officially taken over by the highest Authority in the Church, when *Rome* forbade him to write or teach on philosophical matters. He nevertheless continued the vigorous private circulation of his manuscripts. Here, Prof. Wildiers approves of his disobedience and recommends the fruits of it: *his teachings*, to all.

For a good treatment of the futility of teilhardian attempts at explaining away *duality* and the Real Distinction, I refer interested readers to a little booklet: *Pierre Teilhard de Chardin, Evolution and Christ*, by C. van Til, which first appeared in the May 1966 issue of *The Westminster Theological Journal*, and has been reprinted separately by the Presbyterian and Reformed Publishing Co., Box 185, Nutley 10, New Jersey.

Testimonies as to the extent of Teilhard de Chardin's acceptance in philosophical and theological circles from the thirties to the seventies and to the universality of his influence are innumerable: both in general and of individual theologians. Let me finish with one more, an observation made by a Bishop who attended the Second Vatican Council, the Most Rev. *William Adrian*, Bishop of Nashville, Tennessee. This prelate wrote a penetrating article on this very subject, entitled: *How did it happen?* from which I quote:

"The <u>main issue</u> at the Second Vatican Council was really that of *collegiality,* or the question of how the bishops as a body could somehow rule over the Church, the Pope holding only a Primacy of honour, *not of jurisdiction independent of the bishops.*"

Fr. Wiltgen, in his already mentioned book *The Rhine Flows into the Tiber,* supports the observation made here by Bishop Adrian. Fr. Wiltgen writes on p. 228:

"The most important and dramatic battle which took place at the Second Vatican Council was *not* the widely publicized controversy over Religious Liberty, but the one over *Collegiality,* which happened mostly behind the scenes ..."

Back to Bishop Adrian:

"The liberal bishops knew that, in order to destroy the autocratic power of the Pope and the Curia, they had to stress the idea of *rule by the bishops collectively,* and thus they could overrule the Pope. Also, such a move would overcome the embarrassing doctrine of Papal Infallibility, so inimical to non-Catholics. *But the Pope intervened* and corrected the false doctrines submitted by the bishops ... The European 'periti', (experts!), who really imposed their theories upon the bishops, were themselves deeply imbued with the errors of *Teilhardism* and Situation Ethics, which errors ultimately destroy all Divine Faith and Morality, and all constituted Authority. They make the person the centre and judge of all 'truth' and morality irrespective of what the Church teaches."

But the Pope intervened and corrected ... How long will we be able to hear that happy phrase against such passive resistance, silent timidity and almost murderous ill-will?

This should do to show conclusively the existence of two distinct groups within the kaleidoscopic scene of the pre-Vatican II Catholic Church, prepared on the 11th October, 1962 to present their Catholicism to the judgement of the Church at the opening of the Second Vatican Council.

One group determined to remain within the Tradition of the Church, come what may, willing to make any corrections which their Holy Mother might deem necessary.

The other group outside the Tradition of the Church, determined to prove that, in order to survive and to be relevant to *modern man*, the Church would have to come over to their 'inspiration'.

And in between these two clearly defined groups, the ceaseless ebb and flood of the human caravan-on-the-move, not all that much different from the times when it was viewed with the compassionate eyes of the Son of Man.

Chapter Two

The Filter

Everybody is familiar with Our Lord's parable about the rich having difficulties getting into the Kingdom of Heaven, so much so, that it would be easier for a camel to go through the eye of a needle.

The little story was bound to conjure up in the minds of His listeners the not unfamiliar sight of a rich merchant arriving after dark with his camels at the gates of Jerusalem or some other big city, only to find them closed. Provision was made for such an eventuality in that a traveller could present himself *at the needle's eye*, a little opening in the wall, where he was expected to dismount, unload his beast of burden and pass his possessions through the needle's eye to the guard at the other end. After all that he could, if he could manage it, try to get his camel through the narrow opening as well.

If in times of war or other great upheavals, it was considered necessary to close the gates, the procedure at the needle's eye had the additional advantage of providing the guards with the necessary facilities of checking each caller's intentions and *bona fides* as a traveller or a citizen, by means of a minute inspection of baggage and credentials. If from whatever was presented for inspection some, or most, or even all was refused entry, the caller could either choose to stay outside the wall with his rejected belongings, or else leave them behind and proceed to join his family and friends in-side.

There was, however, a third possibility. He could *bypass* proce-dures and try to force his way in by illegal entry. But then, accord-ing to the words of Our Lord as recorded in John 10:1, it is legiti-mate to consider him a thief and a brigand. (It is important to keep this in mind!).

If these are legitimate associations which Our Lord wanted at-tached to the parable of the needle's eye, then it is not unreasonable to conclude that His Sacred teaching extends to cover any inordi-nate attachment, not only to riches and material possessions, but also to erroneous opinions, prejudices and bad intentions.

In conclusion of this little digression on a familiar theme, I wish to point out that neither the parable nor the proceedings at the needle's eye were meant to be a tribunal, sitting in judgement over personal guilt or innocence. People were free to either pass through the narrow opening, leaving, if necessary, their property behind if it was impossible to bring in or had been refused entry; or refuse to come in, preferring to stay outside with their belongings.

Neither did Vatican II sit in judgement on anybody; but, inexo-rably, it did bring to the surface unacceptable cargo: erroneous opinions and yes, even bad intentions. On each occasion bringing out, in greater clarity, the proper teaching of the Catholic Church on these matters.

Section A
Tradition Itself

There is no doubt that the Sacred Tradition of the Catholic Church passed through Vatican II with flying colours. The Council goes out of its way in its actual wording to firmly base itself on this Tradition; and in innumerable references, both to the earliest documents of the Church and to encyclicals of later Popes as well as to the decisions of other Ecumenical Councils. Vatican II provides us with a rich panorama of its own orthodoxy.

This puts a grave obligation on anyone, not only to accept the Council's declared decision and intention to stay wholly within the Sacred Tradition of the Catholic Church, but also to explain its teaching in the Light of that Tradition.

From the many places in the conciliar documents, where the Council either bases itself explicitly on the teaching of Tradition or declares that its own teaching is in line with this sacred Tradition, we have room here only for a few examples. Then, encouraged by such expressions of genuine orthodoxy, the reader can easily augment the score by a careful reading of the conciliar text.

1. "When we celebrate the Eucharistic Sacrifice we are most closely united to the worship of the heavenly Church, when in the fellowship of communion we honor and remember the glorious Mary ever Virgin, St. Joseph, the holy Apostles and Martyrs and all the Saints. This Sacred Council accepts loyally the venerable Faith of our ancestors in the living communion which exists between us and our brothers who are in the glory of heaven or who are yet to be purified after their death; and it proposes again *the Decrees of* the *Second Council of Nicaea* (A.D. 600), of the *Council of Florence* (1304) and of *the Council of Trent* (1580) ... On the other hand, let the faithful be taught that our communion with these in heaven, provided that it is understood in the full Light of Faith, in no way diminishes the worship of adoration given to God the Father, through Christ in the Spirit: on the contrary, it greatly enriches it."

(*Dogmatic Constitution On the Church*, #50, #51).

2. "Following then in the steps of the Councils of Trent and Vatican I, this Synod wishes to set forth the true doctrine on Divine Revelation and its transmission. For it wants the whole world to hear the summons to Salvation so that through hearing it may believe, through belief it may hope, and through hope it may come to love (St. Augustine) ... *And Tradition transmits in its entirety* the Word of God which has been entrusted to the Apostles by Christ the Lord and the Holy Spirit. It transmits it to the successors of the Apostles so that, enlightened by the Spirit of Truth, they may faithfully preserve, expound and spread it abroad by their preaching. Thus it comes about that the Church does not draw Her certainty about all Revealed Truths from the Holy Scriptures alone. Hence *both Scripture and Tradition* must be accepted and honoured with *equal* feelings of devotion and reverence" (Council of Trent).

(*Dogmatic Constitution On Divine Revelation*, #1, #9.)

3. "In order to satisfy the divine command: 'Make disciples of all the nations', (Mt. 28:19), the Catholic Church must spare no effort in striving 'that the Word of the Lord may speed on and triumph' (2 Thess. 3:1). The Church therefore earnestly urges Her children first of all that 'supplications, prayers, intercessions and thanksgivings be made for all men ... This is good and acceptable in the sight of God our Saviour, who desires all men to be saved and to come to the knowledge of the Truth' (1 Tim. 1:4). *However, in forming their consciences the faithful must pay careful attention to the sacred and certain teaching of the Church. For the Catholic Church is by the Will of God the teacher of Truth.* It is Her duty to proclaim and teach with authority the Truth which is Christ, and at the same time, to declare and confirm *by Her authority* the principles of the moral order which spring from human nature itself. In addition, Christians should approach those who are outside, wisely 'in the Holy Spirit, genuine love, truthful speech' (2 Cor. 6:6-7), and should strive, even to the shedding of their blood, to spread the Light of Life with all confidence and apostolic courage. The disciple has a grave obligation to Christ, his Master, to grow daily in his knowledge of the Truth he has received from Him, to be faithful in announcing it and vigorous in defending it, without having recourse to methods which are contrary to the spirit of the Gospel."

(*Declaration On Religious Liberty* #14).

4. "Nevertheless, our separated brethren, whether considered individually or as communities and churches, are not blessed with that unity which Jesus Christ wished to bestow on all those to whom He has given new birth into one body, and whom He has quickened to newness of life - that unity, which the Holy Scriptures *and the Ancient Tradition of the Church* proclaim. For it is through Christ's Catholic Church *alone*, which is the *universal help towards salvation* that the fullness of the means of salvation can be obtained. It was to the Apostolic College alone, of which Peter is the head, that we believe that Our Lord entrusted all the blessings of the New Covenant, in order to establish on earth the One Body of

Christ into which all those should be fully incorporated who belong in any way to the people of God."

(*Decree On Ecumenism*, #3)

From these, and many other quotations like these, it must become patently clear that, whenever the Council is breaking new ground (Religious Liberty, Ecumenism), she nevertheless is at pains not only to draw inspiration from Tradition, but also to declare that, what is being taught, is truly Catholic. The Modernists, teilhardians and marxist Catholics will not have a bar of this; that is why, in their utter disappointment with Vatican II, they are increasingly turning their attention to means of controlling the government of the Church so they can direct the Church to "Vatican III".

Section B
Teaching Considered Traditional

There is a subtle difference between the official traditional teaching of the Magisterium and the way it was allowed to grow and become accepted and put into practice by Catholics of a given period. We are dealing here with opinions and beliefs which had grown over Tradition and the Deposit of Faith so that they became considered and accepted as part thereof. It is obvious that in this area the Church from time to time must take stock and bring in the necessary corrections.

For example, the watchfulness of the Church in the days of *St. Paul* against any contamination of Jewish teaching on the purity of the Gospel, the watchfulness of the same Church in the days of the

Reformation against reformed inroads into Catholicism, and the watchfulness of the Church of our times against corruption through modernism and Communism could *in practice* be lived by Catholics in a state of animosity against those offending people, which would offend the Universal Law of charity.

The way the Faith is sometimes lived in practice shows how a particular opinion about the implementation of the Faith has grown up, and this may need corrections, not only of the practice itself, but also of the opinion about the manner of implementation. And so we have:

(1) The Catholic Faith;

(2) The authentic Magisterium's teaching about the Faith;

(3) The practice of the Faith;

(4) An opinion about the practice of the Faith.

In the hurly-burly of everyday life, (2) and (4) sometimes get mixed up, and when pre-Vatican II Catholic Life came before the Bar of Vatican II, our Holy Mother the Church acknowledged the essential, *traditional* goodness and truth thereof, but was nevertheless forced to bring in many corrections. And that was not always appreciated or even accepted.

For example, the Church *teaches* that Catholic Faith and Protestant Faith are not the same.

In practice we stay away from each other's services.

Opinion about this practice: it is a good thing that we stay away from each other's services. This opinion became accepted as inviolate.

Archbishop Lefebvre's reaction: "They have changed the Faith! This goes against Tradition ..."

Teilhardian/modernist reaction: "Thank God they have changed the Faith! After all, all faith is the same ..."

Needless to say, neither reaction is right. But if these are the only claims the good Catholics hear, then it is small wonder that their enthusiasm for Vatican II is dampened. Since Vatican II was a Pastoral Council, it was mainly in this area of erroneous opinions about the practice of the Faith that most of the sifting out of otherwise very orthodox Catholics had to be done, and where Catholics were reminded that the fate of the non-Catholics was very much their concern and that this concern demanded the acceptance of the Cross: the Cross of a renewed effort at apostleship.

And it was precisely in *this* area that people like Archbishop *Marcel Lefebvre* refused to give up their 'belongings' and preferred to stay with them outside the walls ... It is no good him claiming he was asked to give up *essentials* to the Faith. Vatican II did nothing of the kind: we all needed training for a tough time ahead, and at times that is not very pleasant. But those of us who did respond, and accepted the discipline and the corrections, very soon started to feel the benefits of true renewal and to obtain the fruits the Church wanted us Catholics to receive from a filial acceptance of the Spirit of the Council. We will return to this in the final chapter of this paper.

Meanwhile, what were some of the 'untouchables' Vatican II held up against the Light, and from which it sifted out what, in that very Light, it considered in need of correction?

(a) The Liturgy

Few of us would have expected that this would have been the very first area where the Council deemed reform necessary. Yet, from the deep-seated revolt that has risen in some quarters of the Church against the Council decisions in reforming the Liturgy, it has come to light that erroneous opinions had become established *around* the Latin Liturgy which stood in need of correction. I have dealt in more detail with these matters in a previous paper: *In Defence of the Novus Ordo Missae of His Holiness Pope Paul VI* in which I showed that objections to the Novus Ordo Missae raised from *history, Tradition, theology* and *Faith* were inadmissible in the Light of True Faith, and only managed to show up the defects in the objectors.

Some may still maintain that the Novus Ordo did not come from Vatican II, but the late Holy Father Pope *Paul VI* has effectively blocked the path of this reasoning on numerous occasions. In this and the following, we are here not dealing with the intentions some Council Fathers may have had in introducing, supporting or rejecting the rich material brought out for discussion, but with the effect these deliberations and decisions had on the Faithful. Or at least <u>were meant</u> to have had.

(b) The Nature of the Catholic Church

For 1900 years the Church has taught authoritatively (including through Vatican II) and the faithful have always believed that the Catholic Church is absolutely necessary for salvation. And so we came to expect that this Council would have stated "... that the Church Christ founded *EXISTS* in the Catholic Church ..." However, the Council, in dealing with this very question, used the word *SUBSISTS*:

"This Church, constituted and organised in the world as a society, *subsists* in the Catholic Church, which is governed by the successor of Peter and by the bishops in union with that successor." (*Lumen Gentium* #8)

This is profound. The Council abstains from telling us what all the Modernists have been at pains to tell us *ad nauseam*, that it is now conciliar teaching, that the bearers of these elements of holiness and truth are *members* of the Catholic Church. But the Council *did* tell us that the possessors of these elements of holiness and truth can thank the Catholic Church of Christ for their existence. The Catholic Church, whilst *subsisting* in the visible society of Catholics, *extends* invisibly further to give to non-Catholics the elements of truth and holiness they may possess, without making the possessors of these elements members.

And so, the Catholic Church is *essential* for non-Catholics so they can possess the graces necessary for salvation. The Modernists have pounced on this word '*subsists*' to claim that the Council has shifted ground on the age-old teaching of the Church so that it now means to include non-Catholics as members. But the conciliar teaching is much more profound than that, and going by the choice of wording used in the text it is obvious that the Council has taught us with much greater clarity *where* the Catholic Church can be *seen to subsist*, and how far She *invisibly extends*.

(c) On True Ecumenism and Religious Liberty

Two further areas of worry for orthodox Catholics can be found in the conciliar teaching on *Ecumenism* and *Religious Liberty*. Mainly because of the false claims made by the Modernists concerning this conciliar teaching. That is why earlier in this paper I have gone to the trouble of quoting words taken from these two Decrees of Vatican II, words which recommend themselves for their orthodoxy and which are the foundation of the teachings to follow.

At present time it is virtually impossible to find out where *in practice* the *true* ecumenism envisaged and taught by Vatican II can be found, since so much of what Vatican II rejected in this area is being proposed as coming from this Council. And the same goes for *true* Religious Liberty: Catholics claiming for themselves a *freedom of conscience* which is tantamount to rejecting Catholic Faith in favour of an imaginary new-found 'freedom'. But not all the trouble comes from the false claims made in these areas: much of it stems from erroneous convictions adopted by pre-conciliar Catholics who used the safety of their ignorance as a pretext and excuse for aloofness and inaction.

To be reminded of one's ecumenical obligations is painful, and the use made everywhere of the false ecumenism and the bogus 'freedom of conscience' by the teilhardians, marxists and Modernists must not deter us to put into practice what Vatican II taught us with authority and truthfulness in these matters.

These few examples must suffice to show us that, irrespective of rampant falsehoods made available everywhere to warp the impact

of Vatican II, which may have frightened off orthodox Catholics,
these Catholics are thereby not excused from looking into themselves to see if there is something within themselves which Vatican
II sifted out but which they refuse to give up, and which is the real
reason why they allow a mistrust of the Council to continue in
their lives. For if this is the case, then they miss out on enormous
graces which the Cross of Vatican II was meant to unleash in their
lives and in the lives of the souls entrusted to their care ...

Section C
Teilhardian Modernism

If we can be sure of one thing, it is that *Teilhardian Modernism
and Evolution* got blocked by the Sacred Council in no uncertain
way. Nothing of this was allowed through. It is absolutely impossible to maintain that, even if force was used on the text, the sacred
documents refer - however remotely - to an evolutionary spirit.
Everything is solid, traditional language. The examples one can
choose are myriad:

1. "For it is the Liturgy through which, especially in the Divine
Sacrifice of the Eucharist 'the work of our redemption is accom-
plished' (Hebr. 13:14), and it is through the Liturgy especially that
the faithful are enabled to express in their lives and manifest to
others the mystery of Christ and the real nature of the true Church.
The Church is essentially both human and divine, visible but en-
dowed with invisible realities ... so constituted that in Her the human is directed toward and subordinated to the Divine, the visible
to the invisible ..."

This clearly establishes, from the opening paragraph of the First Document promulgated: *The Constitution on the Sacred Liturgy*, the traditional acceptance of the Real Distinction between the natural and the supernatural rejected by the teilhardians. The Council accepts Sacrifice, Redemption, the Eucharistic Sacrifice, all unacceptable to the reigning Modernists as well as being unobtainable by mere human efforts, (such as 'belief' in evolution).

2. "God Who wills that all men be saved and come to the knowledge of the truth, (1. Tim. 2:4) ... when the fullness of time had come, sent His Son, the Word made flesh, anointed by the Holy Spirit, to preach the Gospel to the poor, to heal the contrite of heart, to be a bodily and spiritual medicine: the Mediator between God and man. For His Humanity, united with the Person of the Word, was the instrument of our salvation. In Christ the perfect achievement of our reconciliation came forth and the fullness of Divine Worship was given to us." (Liturgy #5)

No trace of modernism or evolution here: Real Distinction between God and man taught, divinity of Christ acclaimed, the fact that Christ was and is a Divine Person stressed, etc.

3. "Before men can come to the liturgy, they must be called to Faith and to conversion ... So the Church announces the good tidings of salvation to those who do not believe so that all men may come to the knowledge of the one true God, and Jesus Christ Whom He has sent and may be converted from their ways, doing penance." (Liturgy #9)

No 'inter-communion' here. 'Penance' is not admitted in an evolutionary system, since in such a system *sin* does not exist, only mistakes.

4. "To believers also the Church must ever preach Faith and Penance; She must prepare them for the Sacraments ... thus making it clear that Christ's faithful, *though not of this world*, are to be the lights of the world and are to glorify the Father before men." (Liturgy #9)

In an evolutionary system, the faithful would be part of the evolving world like everybody else.

5. "From the Liturgy, therefore, and especially from the Eucharist, *Grace* is poured forth upon us as from a fountain ..."

A Church which still holds fast to the teaching of the existence of 'grace' as something 'that flows from a fountain' is certainly not a Church that is inspired by modernism and 'evolution'.

6. "The *Catholic Church* was founded by Christ Our Lord to bring salvation to all men ... The second question bears on the relation between the rights of art - to use a current expression - and the moral law. The controversies to which this problem increasingly gives rise frequently trace their origin to an erroneous understanding either of ethics or of aesthetics. The Council proclaims that all must accept *the Absolute Primacy of the Objective Moral Order.* It alone is superior to, and is capable of harmonizing, all forms of human activity, not excepting art, no matter how noble in themselves. Only the Moral Order touches Man in the totality of his being as God's rational creature, called to a Supernatural Destiny. If the moral order is fully and faithfully observed, it leads man to full perfection and happiness."

(*Decree on Social Communications* #3, #6)

So the Council still believes in, and teaches the existence of, *absolutes*: an absolute moral order of Supernatural origin, coming from outside man i.e. from man's Creator, and which is written in his totality as creature, as a rational creature. With this clear teaching, the Council unequivocally rejects *situation ethics* and the *primacy of a subjective moral code* as is taught by Kohlberg and innumerable 'catholic' moralists.

7. "Deep within his conscience man discovers a law *which he has not laid upon himself but which he must obey ... For man has in his heart a law inscribed by God.* His dignity lies in observing this law, and by it he will be judged ... Since human freedom has been weakened by *sin*, it is only by the help of God's *grace* that man can give his actions their full and proper relationship to God."

(*Church in the Modern World* #16, #17)

So the Council sticks to her teaching about obedience to a transcending, absolute and universal moral law, written by God in man's heart, and that God's grace is needed to keep that law.

8. "Although set by God in a state of rectitude, man, enticed by the Evil One, abused his freedom at the very start of history. He lifted himself against God and sought to attain his goal apart from Him."

(*Church in the Modern World* #13)

9. "At that moment (i.e. of the Church's glorious completion), as the Fathers put it, all the just from the time of Adam, 'from Abel, the just one, to the last of the elect' (*St. Gregory the Great, St. Augustine, St. John Damascene*), will be gathered together, with the Father, in the Universal Church."

(*Lumen Gentium* #2)

10. "In reality it is only in the mystery of the Word made flesh that the mystery of man truly becomes clear. For Adam, the first man, was a type of Him Who was to come, Christ the Lord, Christ the new Adam ... He Who is 'the image of the invisible God', is Himself the perfect Man who has restored in the children of Adam that likeness to God which had been disfigured ever since the first sin."

(*Church in the Modern World* #22.)

These last three are the final blow to evolution, teilhardism and modernism: this sustained and orthodox teaching on *Original Sin* and *our First Parents*.

This must do to show by overwhelming evidence that, no matter where one opens the Conciliar documents, one will always find authentic teaching of the Catholic Church of Tradition and the total absence of any trace of teilhardian evolution: neo and systematic modernism. Whatever was brought into the Council tainted by evolution and modernism was ruthlessly sifted out and rejected.

This means that, if the post-Conciliar Church became saturated with the heresies of Modernism, they did not come from this Council nor from the Catholic Church. The harbingers of these evils forced their way into the sheepfold, not through the Gate, but through some other way. (John 10:1).

Chapter Three

The Bypass

In Chapter One we were made aware of the existence of a massive body of Western elite, which had adopted a philosophy of which Communism is one logical expression.

We accepted the fact that this body of the "new order intellectuals" of necessity contained a very large slice of Catholic intelligentsia since it is made up of people who have uprooted themselves from the Catholic Tradition which lies at the foundation of the European Civilization.

A study of the *philosophy* of this "*new order*" and of the "*Nouvelle Théologie*" of Prof. N. M. Wildiers confirms our strong suspicion that, inevitably, it has, as its chief characteristic, Teilhard's evolutionary principle of *Sameness and Identity* since it broke away from the age-old Catholic Philosophy which, even long before *St. Thomas Aquinas*, had as its foundation principle the *Real Distinction* between God and Creation and between matter and spirit.

But it was not until His Holiness Pope Pius XI illuminated our natural understanding of these things with the supernatural insights of Faith, when, in his celebrated encyclical against Atheistic Communism, he taught us with the force of the highest teaching authority in the Church *that Communism is absolutely contrary to the Natural Law itself and that it is rooted in evolution which abolishes the real distinction between God and matter, between the Crea-*

tor and the creature, between the natural and the Supernatural. Therefore, whoever accepts a *new order* and a *new philosophy* <u>of which Communism is a logical expression and a psychological and emotional 'blood brother'</u>, must have embraced a philosophy absolutely contrary to Natural Law itself and which must be rooted in evolution for Communism to be able to be a logical and emotional expression of it.

We do know that the Western Catholic intelligentsia *has* adopted *a philosophy of evolution*: Teilhardism, which *has* rejected Thomism and the Real Distinction principle, and which *does have* as its starting point the totally inadmissible principle of identity and sameness of everything in the one plane: evolution.

(Cf. Teilhard de Chardin in all his works, but especially in his 1922 paper against Original Sin, his 1929 paper *The Human Sense*, his books *The Phenomenon of Man* and *The divine Milieu* and in his 1947 paper, his third against Original Sin).

We further know that this philosophy, and the "Nouvelle Théologie" (Dutch 'catechism'!) to which it gave birth, were forcefully and persistently presented at the Second Vatican Council 'as genuine expressions of Catholicism' only to be equally forcefully and persistently filtered out and rejected through the direct protection by the Holy Spirit.

As we saw, there is not a trace of Modernism or evolution in any Council document, notwithstanding the totally misleading picture painted by people like *Michael Davies* who in his infamous book *Pope John's Council* contrives to 'prove' his erroneous preconceived idea that, since there was a marked influence of *the Rhine* at the Council, it had to prevail ... The Holy Spirit only used the miserable attempts by the 'Rhine' group to shape the Cross necessary for the purification and correction of orthodox Catholics, but not for the formulation of doctrine contrary to Traditional Teaching.

And since Michael Davies and his group of 'Tridentiners' reject this Cross in preference to the sterile suffering of disobedience and schism, they reject the Council which offered this Cross in Name of Our Holy Mother the Church for the salvation of the world.

They have rejected this Cross and this Sacred Council at their peril. For with their action they have also rejected the Supernatural Light so necessary to make this Cross meaningful. And they have led thousands astray with their endless prattle at the base of the **Towering Rock of Peter**, which they have now declared and pointed out *as a shipping hazard* to the delight of the Modernists. For what more could the Modernists hope for than that, at the very time of the most concentrated attack on the foundations of the Catholic Church and the Papacy, the so-called 'injustices', which the Tridentiners imagine have been meted out to them, have made ordinary Catholics silent and sullen in the defence of the Council and the Papacy, because of the totally mistaken idea that these devilish attacks could come from the Church Herself, a church-gone-wrong.

Theirs is a defamation of the Majesty of God, which they will come to regret. At the very moment that the Catholic Church is fighting the battle of Her life for Her credibility and even for Her visible presence amongst us, these people believe and preach that, at the most crucial moment of the Catholic Church's long history, God gave to His Church a Council which is so unsure and unsound that it is to be ignored and rejected. And gave us a Holy Father

Pope *Paul VI* 'heretical enough' to implement these unsure and unsound teachings of the Council. *Perish the thought ...!*

What, then, is at stake?

At stake is the credibility and the visible presence of the Catholic Church amongst us here on earth. Ever since the Sacred Council, the Modernists and Marxists have ravaged our Holy Mother the Catholic Church and torn Her apart. Their philosophy and theology, their evolution and heresies were thrown out by the Church in Vatican II in no uncertain manner. That should have been the end of the story. That it is *not* shows that, in their absolute determination to destroy every vestige of the Catholic Church, *A BYPASS HAD TO BE FOUND.*

And found it was ...

What, then, is this fools-gold of tantalising beauty which is considered so valuable that our modernistic Catholic elite and intelligentsia has sold everything, including its intellectual honesty and even its birthright to Everlasting Life in order to possess it? In the colossal pretence that, through them, the Holy Church is now in bondage to acknowledge the value of their mesmerising 'vision'?

What is considered so important for the introduction into the Catholic fold, that, even after its ignominious rejection at the Council, *a detour simply had to be found* in order to introduce it at all cost? To *force* it on us?

Is it evolution?

No it is not. Nobody believes in evolution. Teilhardian evolution is absurd. But it is the only syringe that contains the deadly poison, the lethal *drug* ... After the injection, the empty syringe is useless and is discarded ...

Is it Existentialism?

No, it is not. Existentialism is only a system of thought to give bogus existences to things that do not exist, preventing a serious study of the nature of the contraband. But here again, although, useless in itself, existentialism is nevertheless *indispensable as a mask* and a *wrapping* to hide the murderous face of the one that holds the deadly weapon ...

No, the solution to solving the riddle of what is driving our Modernists will have to be found in something far more mundane and down-to-earth. In something that is lure enough to make people subordinate everything else to it in their unholy quest for its acquisition.

What did *Bishop William Adrian* of Nashville, Tennessee, say was the **main** issue at the Second Vatican Council? Did he not say:

"The main issue at the Second Vatican Council was really that of *collegiality,* or the question of how the bishops as a body could somehow rule over the Church, the Pope holding only a Primacy of honour, *not of jurisdiction independent of the bishops?*"

And did *Fr. Wiltgen* in his book *The Rhine flows into the Tiber* not agree with him in these words:

"The most important and dramatic battle which took place at the Second Vatican Council was *not* the widely publicized controversy over Religious Liberty, but the one over *Collegiality*, which happened mostly behind the scenes ..."

Thus the name of the game is **POWER**. Hunger for *Power to Control* ...

But naked aggression too early displayed is resisted and squashed. It is better to use something that is subtle but eminently effective, something that can even make people excited enough to make this power-to-control seem necessary, so it becomes acceptable without unnecessary violence. Not before it becomes *popular* to persecute. <u>And when will that be?</u>

According to the American sociologist *H. Blumer* ("Collective Behavior" in *Principles of Sociology*, A. M. Lee edition, New York, 1951, pp. 165-222), **four** fundamental factors are important for the success of a new, social movement:

First, a **general uneasiness** in which men are responsive to a new appeal;

Second, a **popular rising**, in which all are agreed as to the sources of the difficulty and in which the goals of the movement are clearly defined;

Third, **indoctrination**, i.e. the creation of a body of dogmas and a vanguard of adherents to disseminate them; and

Fourth, **institutionalization** which is necessary in order to realize the goals of the movement.

We could not wish for a better *birth certificate* of the forthcoming One-World 'Church' predicted and foreseen by His Holiness Pope *St. Pius X* already in 1910.

- **EVOLUTION** has created a world-wide *uneasiness* with regard to Christianity and especially with regard to the Catholic Church in Her prohibitions against Teilhard de Chardin.
- **ECUMENISM** has become *the popular uprising* in which all are asked to agree that "the old Church" is the source of the

difficulty. The Catholic Church with Her claim to uniqueness has kept us all divided.

- **MODERNISM** with its 'group dynamics', 'sensitivity training' and 'audacity', is meant to release the pent-up feelings
  of frustration and will consolidate these vague notions into
  "dogmas of reasonableness" by indoctrination, by which
  Catholics who refuse to go along with it can be singled out
  as queer, unreasonable splitters; and finally the new,

- **ONE-WORLD CHURCH** of Ecumenism and Unity will
  institutionalize it all on a world wide scale in the name of
  the World Council of Churches and the Holy Spirit ...

Only then will it be popular to persecute, in the name of world
unity and in the name of the Holy Spirit, all those who will not
conform and refuse admission.

With such global power at stake, the Modernists simply could
not accept the defeat received in the Second Vatican Council. For
they knew that *underneath* evolution and existentialism, and *inside*
the syringe and the masquerading wrapping, lies hidden the *one*
ingredient vital to the success of their whole power struggle and
global conquest:

"The Philosophy of Sameness", the "Principle of Identity"

For the success of the whole movement it is imperative that millions of lukewarm, materialistic, browned-off Catholics make their
entry into the new, man-made *Church of Darkness* to create the
illusion that the Catholic Church Herself has entered under their
powerful guidance.

For this to happen the false ecumenism is absolutely essential since it possesses the *one* ingredient necessary for success: this Principle of Sameness. Divisions in Christianity are only apparent: deep down, all Christians are the same ... Global unification requests as a necessary prerequisite: *pluralism in doctrine* ("it is all the same what you believe"), which in turn requires the abolition of Catholic Dogma (e.g. the Assumption), since it is precisely this *pluralism-in-doctrine* which gives the illusion of "sameness for all". It is all the same if you believe in Mary's Assumption or not; your beliefs are your personal affair as long as you do not believe in absolutes: Absolute Truth and an Absolute Moral Code.

For global unification also demands *pluralism-in-morality,* so morality can become adaptable to situations which is incompatible with an absolute moral code: the Ten Commandments. It is all the same, really, if you practise abortion or not, as long as you do not declare anything absolute except *relativity in morals.*

This principle of sameness and identity between the natural and the supernatural, between 'relative' and 'absolute' does, of course, not exist: it has only the appearance, the illusion, of existence: a veritable *existentialist* existence. But it has been laid at the root and heart of Modernism so much so, that **no Modernist**, be he Hans Kung, Karl Rahner, Fr. Arnold Hogan or Sr. Peter Traviss; no architect of the "Church of Darkness", no agent of the false ecumenism, can open his or her mouth, *however cautiously*, without being instantly recognised by it. And this by the saving Will of God, Who is asking a veritable Cross from His followers at the present time, ***but not deception ...***

This 'philosophy of sameness and identity' is the fundamental and eternal enemy of the Real Distinction, and here, at the core of the battle for the safeguarding of the Real Distinction, the Catholics have their most Powerful Ally: *Transubstantiation*, or Christ Himself in the Blessed Eucharist. For here, *the Real Distinction comes to Life*; here it is Lived; here it becomes elevated to Dogma: eternally true, the Word of God Himself. What was bread *before* the Consecration ceases to be bread *after* it, and a totally new Substance, totally and Really Distinct from the substance of bread, takes its place: the Body of Our Lord Jesus Christ.

No wonder, then, that the fury of Hell on earth: Modernism, has raised its greatest howl and outcry against this most sacred Dogma of the Catholic Church. For if **this** Real Distinction is allowed to remain, **all** real distinctions are saved and kept in place, and the 'philosophy of sameness' is doomed.

In one of the worst books ever printed in defence of Modernism: *What are the theologians saying?*, in which the compiler, one Monika Hellwig, allows Satan to spew his venom over the sacred teaching of the Church, the Dogma of Transubstantiation is mercilessly attacked in hatred:

"The Pope's personal judgement was that for most adult Catholics today the full spiritual meaning of the Eucharist is carried in the word transubstantiation. Many theologians hope (because the word is still so offensive to devout Protestant Christians, and because younger Catholics are quite confused by it) that one day it will slide out of the official formulations into history, along with transfiguration and transformation, as just one way of describing an elusive and many-faceted mystery".

After having attacked the teaching of Pope Paul VI in his jewel *Mystery of Faith* with all the lies and cunning she is capable of, this is the final summing up: "*Pope Paul's personal judgement*"! After the Pontiff had gone out of his way to put before us *infallible teaching* held by the Catholic Church throughout the ages, and had become the *third* Pope in history to declare *Transubstantiation* a Dogma of the Church, as such defined by the *Council of Trent*.

"*Sliding into history and oblivion ...*" against the solemn teaching of this same Pontiff in #9 of the same encyclical:

"Indeed we are aware of the fact that, among those who deal with this Most Holy Mystery in written or spoken word, there are some who with reference to the *Dogma of Transubstantiation* spread abroad opinions which disturb the faithful and fill their minds with no little confusion about matters of Faith. It is as if everyone were permitted *to consign to oblivion* doctrine already *defined* by the Church, or else interpret it in such a way as to weaken the genuine meaning of the words or the recognised force of the concepts involved".

On the testimony of the Holy Father here, if the theologians are really saying what Hellwig tells us they are saying (and there is plenty of evidence in support of Hellwig's claims), then what the Modernists are talking about is how to abort our Catholic Faith, and it is obvious that such attempts and such teaching can only come into the sheepfold by devious means: *by a detour bypassing Vatican II.* Karl Rahner gets pride of place in Hellwig's book; his thoughts and teachings are expressed in 5 out of the 10 essays. In one of them, on 'grace', he is bracketed with 'theologian' Teilhard de Chardin.

"The Gospel of the Church of Darkness" as expressed in books like *What are the theologians saying?* and *Toward Vatican III* is loud and clear: "See for yourself how reasonable the philosophy of sameness is, how reasonable our solutions are, against the unreasonabless of Catholic Dogma and the Real Distinction!" And against this, all that our good Catholics have to do is to renew their Supernatural, Infused, Divine and Catholic Faith in Transubstantiation: *the Dogma that has canonized the Real Distinction. ...*

Chapter Four

"... For wide is the road that leads to perdition, and many take it ..." (Matt. 7:23)

Now that we are convinced of the *fact* and the *reasons* why it is 'full speed ahead' for the Modernists after Vatican II, it would be very instructive to draw the attention of the reader to some very interesting bits and pieces of information, which reveal the existence of a detour: a network of channels and pipelines used by the religious leaders of the world to bypass the Magisterium of the Catholic Church, at the same time that they attempt to involve the Church with the trafficking along the doctrinal drug trails, unceasingly preparing for the day when the "*doctrine*" of their own making will be taught by a "*church*" of their own making, approved by a "*pope*" of their own making, one that may look like the Lamb but speaks like the Dragon (Apoc. 13:11).

Some of this evidence clearly points to conclusions reached or decisions taken prior to, or at the latest concurrent with, the Second Vatican Council. This means that neither these decisions and conclusions nor the 'teachings' they contain can in any way be traced to the 'inspiration' and 'insights' of Vatican II. A few examples will be helpful.

1. It may all be very ecumenical and 'Christ-like' of His Grace, Archbishop Frank Little of Melbourne, Australia, to ask for, and obtain, from his Senate of Priests permission to join the Victorian branch of the World Council of Churches, but what follows has been officially stated in reports from a WCC organised World Conference, *The Eighth Conference on World Missions* in Bangkok, 1973.

In 1974 there appeared on the world scene an English translation of an incredible German book, written by a Lutheran Doctor in Theology, which book dispelled any doubts many may still have about the 'religious' future of the world. The title of the book is *Bangkok 73*, and its author is Prof. Peter Beyerhaus. If anyone still needs convincing that Modernism is conceived in Hell, this book will achieve that.

Prof. Beyerhaus is one of that rare breed of international theologians still wholly uncontaminated by Modernism, and his book *Bangkok 73* is an eyewitness account of what actually took place before *and* at the 8th Conference on World Mission, held at Bangkok in 1973, under the auspices of the World Council of Churches. The title of this World Conference on Missions was - significantly enough – "*Salvation Today*".

In his book Prof. Beyerhaus explains to us the unbelievable but *total* contradiction that took place at the Conference: how 326 serious, mission-minded delegates can come together to study the *advance* of global missionary activity, and can come out with the exact opposite: calling for a *halt*, a *moratorium* on missionary activity, **thinking that they were still the <u>same</u> people, and that they were doing God and the missions a good turn ..!**

In this contradiction lies the most accurate description one could ever hope to give of Modernism and all its off-shoots, expressing in its brevity the most fundamental objection the Holy Church could ever have against it.

Prof. Beyerhaus meets the issue head-on. "*The true key*", he says "*to the planning of the course and to the full understanding of the Bangkok Conference itself lies in the professed 'equation' between a systematically staged socio-psychological experiment* (i.e group-dynamics: 'brainwashing') *and the action of the Holy Spirit*".

And the professor then sets out to show from every angle and with a welter of detail how this perversion "*of equating brainwashing with the Holy Spirit*" was carried out. Nothing was left to chance! Even the objection that such an exercise is impossible is squarely met. The poor delegates did not have a chance from the word go. Why? ***Because they became involved!***

And judging by the innumerable Catholics who now believe the opposite of what the Church taught us before, who no longer can tell the difference between Catholic Faith and any other faith, and who think that "being on the pill" and accepting Church teaching can go together: the experiment did not stop at Bangkok, but has swept the world.

In describing all the aspects of how the basic rules of brainwashing were applied at Bangkok, Prof. Beyerhaus lays bare *the* most crucial, central brand-mark of Modernism, stamped on it by the inventors of the 'philosophy of sameness' "*the complete mutual openness, so that people can expose their vulnerability **without questioning***". He quotes *Dr. Hoffmann* in an interview for the South West German Radio:

"We hope that there are enough people here who are vulnerable and who will let themselves be wounded, so that they can hear the strange things and the unheard of things which have never yet been heard that others will say to them ..."

And Prof. Beyerhaus' comment:

"This meant that we should be ready to call all the convictions in question, and all the presuppositions we brought with us, and even that we should abandon them in order to open ourselves up to 'unheard of things', *perhaps even that which contradicts our Christian Faith ...!*"

When the white delegates *"became involved"* and accepted this condition, and were subsequently confronted by the coloured delegates with all the evils of 'colonialism' and with the 'evils of missionary activities carried out in name of colonialism', the stony-faced white delegates were eventually made to feel so crushed that they not only became ashamed of their colour, but ever so much more importantly for the marxists staging the show (*and for Satan behind them*) became ashamed of their Christian religion. And to make up for the evils done, they voted for the moratorium on mission activity.

The reader is now sufficiently up-to-date with the thrust and the mechanics of this "Eighth Conference on World Missions" to grasp what Prof. Beyerhaus is saying on the reports that emanated from it.

"These reports sketch the blurred contours of an approaching unified religion in which Christianity contributes merely some formal suggestions for the general ideas of God, religion and salvation. Inasmuch as the name of Christ **in the sense of the Cosmic Christology promulgated at New Delhi** (1961), is still retained, all this is a typical, alluring example of syncretism". (p. 53)

So the World Council of Churches has adopted the "*cosmic christ*" of Teilhard de Chardin, that evolutionary figment of a feverish imagination ...

One more report from Prof. Beyerhaus' book, this one on '*communal prayer*':

"You were a poor Mexican baptized by the Holy Spirit and the blood of the Lamb. ... I rejoice with you, my brother."

"You were an intellectual Chinese who broke through the barrier between yourself and the dung-smelling peasant. ...I rejoice with you, my brother."

"You found all the traditional language meaningless and became 'an atheist by the grace of God'. ... I rejoice with you, my brother".

"Thus for the first time in the history of Christianity, an ecumenical conference has here joined in rejoicing over the fact that someone had become an atheist and that even 'by the grace of God' ..." (p. 73).

Are we allowed to wonder how Archbishop F. Little of Melbourne and bishop R. Mulkearns from the diocese of Ballarat would fare in any ecumenical gathering where, because of their membership of the World Council of Churches, they would be asked to join in and extol 'beatitudes' which reject a dung-smelling peasant by Christianity, but rejoice over someone becoming an atheist "by the grace of God ..."

It is all very well for bishops to claim 'Vatican II ecumenism' on their side to justify association with the World Council of Churches, but the New Delhi World Conference of the WCC, in which the 'Cosmic Christ of Teilhard de Chardin' was officially adopted when it adopted his "cosmic Christology", happened to take place in 1961, and so can only be reached by a detour, bypassing Vatican II, since Vatican II **blocked** teilhardism and filtered it out for rejection.

And so *no ecumenism* can be claimed by any Catholic bishop, who would link his (Arch)diocese with teilhardian heresies and syncretism through his association with the World Council of Churches. Not only would membership stifle all protest against the blatant display of marxism on the World Council as witnessed by the extolling of atheism, but it would furthermore make Catholics agreeable to the formulations of such policies, a fact to which the reports of **all** the World Conferences of the WCC since the New Delhi debacle have testified: Uppsala, Kyoto, Louvain, and beyond.

2. From what we read in so-called 'official documents', many Religious appear to be firmly convinced, that their blatantly modernistic ideas of the *Religious Vows* can be traced to Vatican II. So was one Sr. Kelly recently allowed to write in the Melbourne diocesan paper *The Advocate* (May 4, 1978) that (luckily for the good nuns): "Canon Law on Religious mostly good". In the body of the article under this headline she enlightened us on the following:

"Participants also discussed changing interpretations of the religious Vows of poverty, chastity and obedience."

For 2000 years they have always meant only one thing. Now hear how this timeless meaning is being changed into its opposite and, *through the philosophy of sameness*, still held up to us as being the same.

"Formerly (i.e. for 2000 years, ever since the days of Our Lady and Her Son) *poverty* meant: *do without*, Sr. Kelly said. Now it means: transcend material things. *Chastity* meant: *Stay away from*.

Now it means: loving availability of service. *Obedience* meant: *Do not do this or that.* Now it means: mutuality (between community leader and member) in discerning the Father's will."

If this cannot be traced to the Second Vatican Council, although strongly implied here, then where does it come from?

During the Second Vatican Council a book appeared entitled: *Generation of the Third Eye,* in which some 20 leading American Catholics on the sunny side of 40 were asked to write down candidly their experiences as Catholics and what they hoped the Council would change. This book is a marvellous example of the **'bypass'** we are talking about here, illustrating the modernism quite rampant in 'intellectual Catholic circles' at that time, and what they expected would eventually be able to be traced back to the Council. A Nun was also asked to write her thoughts on the matter, and here is part of what she had to say:

"Our community is going through a phase of Karl Rahner spirituality and these past few months I have been meditating on a *Cross Currents* reprint of his *Reflections on Obedience.* Here, with his characteristic gift of brushing away the non-essential, Rahner finds the meaning of religious obedience in 'the permanent binding of oneself to a definite mode of life' ... Obedience, then, is by no means to be understood as a mere abstract readiness to do the will of another ..."

(It may help if the reader knows that this dear soul is, amongst other things, (don't laugh!) a member of the society for *Existential Phenomenology* ... she continues):

"As a nun I am solidly behind Card. Suenens' exhortation that the religious orders of women be represented at the Council and -

even more importantly - that they participate actively in the revision of Canon Law, *which will enable them to make needed changes in their own Constitutions ...*"

It appears to me that there is a great similarity between the Sr. Kelly mentality and that of the '*Nun in the bypass*' who could not trace her ideas to the Second Vatican Council. Instead, she claims to be greatly inspired by a theologian who has thrown his enormous weight behind the teilhardian theology of the rejection of Original Sin, supporting the master's advocacy of polygenism 'even on scientific grounds'!, but not without disastrous effects to his reputation.

What Fr. Rahner "*sweeps away in those articles with his characteristic gift*" is very essential to Dogma and Catholic Faith, and was not supported by Vatican II. Furthermore, the art of 'sticking to one's lifestyle' has nothing to do with the Vow of Obedience, but can quite easily have a lot to do with 'doing your own thing', pigheadedness, and worse ...

If this is the sound of some of the earlier 'Catholic' voices-in-the-bypass, what were the non-Catholics encouraged to say?

3. The following is taken from a book called *The Coming World Church* by a group of Protestant scholars, who gathered their evidence from various existing documents on the activities of the World Council of Churches. It was printed in 1963 and so was researched and compiled some years *before Vatican II*. Obviously, the Second Vatican Council does not inspire either the teaching reported herein, or the theories advanced, or the practices put into operation. So *no bishop* may claim inspiration from Vatican II, if he contemplates joining up with the world body described in this book: the World Council of Churches.

"*Dr. G. Bromley Oxnam* is credited with having prepared the blueprints for both the National Council of Churches (American) and the WCC. He thoroughly understood the role they would play in achieving his dream of '*The coming Great Church*'."

(Now listen carefully to what this 'dream' is based on):

"In his book *On the Rock*, this late great ecumenist **bypassed** all the basic tenets of evangelical Christian doctrine, and called for the abandonment of all traditional and organizational barriers to church union. He proposed first to bring about inclusive coopera-tive Protestant action in the realm of church functions. Next he would create an ecumenical ministry. The bishop himself said he would be gladly re-ordained under this system. He declared:

'I would gladly kneel in a service of mutual sharing in which the blessings of the different ordinations might be **symbolically** con-ferred upon me'."

Then Oxnam enlarges the picture:

"United actions in many fields would follow ... missions ... edu-cation ... united theological seminaries ... the ministers of the church. The union of American christianity would electrify the world and accelerate the trend towards union in every continent. 'Finally' said the bishop, 'it will be possible to kneel before a com-mon altar with the Roman Catholic Church, beg forgiveness of the Christ for disunity and sharing the bread and wine of holy com-munion, rise in his Spirit to form the Holy Catholic Church to which all Christians may belong'."

If this is the theory, then (still quoting from the same book) *what is the practice?*

"In America this ecumenical church is being built through the actions of Councils affiliated with the National Council of Churches, (NCC, like the one existing in Australia) and in mergers of various denominations. The Northern California Council of Churches will make a good example. A local Council has a *Comity Committee* which has assigned certain territories to certain denominations *to the exclusion of all others.* Before any new church can be established, permit must be secured (*coercion*) from the local Council of Churches. City planning commissions and even national housing administrators are advised that *maverick churches*, that is, those that do not bear the stamp of Council approval, should not be allowed to construct buildings in areas under their control."

And now comes the crunch ...

"All pastors of Churches which have been allocated specific territories by the Comity Commission are advised that they represent not only their own denomination but also *the Ecumenical church.* They are required to emphasize the teachings **which their denominations share with the rest of Christendom.** In other words, the ecumenical church already exists in the thinking of the Council, as does an ecumenical ministry, with all planning for the future motivated by a determination to achieve *One Church for One World.*"

This leaves in clarity as with regard to both theory and practice nothing to be desired.

It is becoming pretty obvious that the Catholic Church which neither can nor will go along with this sort of ecumenism, as it is impossible to bind Her to teach only what is shared by the rest of 'christendom', is heading for the classification of a *"maverick Church"* by the unanimous decision of all the churches and councils which DO go along with it, *including the 'Catholic' slice that joined them* ... It is quite likely that in the years to come many bishops of the Roman Catholic Church will start contemplating the step which has been taken here in the Archdiocese of Melbourne and its suffragan diocese of Ballarat, and will take their dioceses within the Council of Churches, with the inevitable consequences as described here, including that they will leave the Catholics who do not want to join up to fend for themselves as best they can. The American experience (already dating from 1963) is a sobering thought for all of us.

A few pages back the question was asked:

"When will it be popular to start persecuting?"

Here is one answer:

- When individual Catholics have been *effectively* isolated by this type of action.
- When they are *not* allowed to talk about, or teach, the doctrines not shared by the rest of Christendom.
- When they are *only* allowed to stress the 'cosmic christ' of the WCC, the one shared by all the denominations.
- When they are requested to take "communion" from an ecumenical minister whose Sunday it happens to be.
- And when they refuse to go along with any of this ...

It is interesting to see in this context what, by Divine Revelation, we know will happen; and what St. John described in the 13th chapter of the Book of Revelation: how the second beast (or the false prophet) which looks like the Lamb but speaks like the Dragon will do everything in its power to use the religious unity of the world to obtain the political unity under the first beast. He also tells us that *"the whole world will run after the beast"*. In support of this interpretation we quote here the official teaching of Pope St. Pius X who wrote in 1910:

"... for the establishment of a One-World 'Church' which shall have neither dogma nor hierarchy, neither discipline of the mind nor curb on the passions, and which, under the pretext of freedom and human dignity, will bring back to the world the reign of legalised cunning and brute force and the oppression of the weak, and of all those who toil and suffer."

Same thing. Only this time the information is raised above the level of private interpretation of Scripture to the authentic voice of the Magisterium. And we can be sure of one thing: the 'ecumenism' and practices of the One-World 'Church', held up here by Pope *St. Pius X* as a warning for us, can never be traced back to Vatican II. Whoever contemplates joining up with such a global agglomerate, can only do so on the inspiration of the *bypass* where the rejects of Vatican II congregate...

Chapter Five

"The Good Will Be Martyred ..."
(Our Blessed Lady at Fatima)

The stakes are high ...

"The goal of the boldest ecumenical thinkers and leaders has grown increasingly clear: to construct a world community embracing all races, classes, religions and political systems, united as far as possible under a common world government whose business will be the establishment of world peace. It is hoped that *a Universal Church will be able to pave the way successfully for a Universal Government.*"

This comes so close to what St. John wrote to us in his Book of Revelation about "the second beast doing everything in its power to subjugate the whole world to the tyranny of the first beast", that the question is legitimate: "Is Prof. Peter Beyerhaus indulging here in 'private interpretation of Scripture', *or is this an exercise in sheer clear thinking from available evidence*? He continues:

"Such a universal church would, however, not only be trans-confessional, it would also be unconditionally open to partnership with other religions and ideologies. The former General Secretary of the WCC, *Eugene Carson Blake*, declared in October, 1970 at the World Conference of Religions for Peace, in *Kyoto*, Japan, that the church unity for which the WCC strives, is only a first step on the way to the ultimate goal of a united mankind ... In the advocates of the ecumenical movement we are encountering today, we find a passionate *religious-political* view of missions, whose ardor, fanned to a new high at *Bangkok*, refuses to let any objections keep it from its goal.

If anyone does stand in the way,

- he is wooed in a friendly manner,
- simply passed over as unimportant, or, if these methods are not effective,
- wrathfully attacked ..."

(Prof. P. Beyerhaus in *Bangkok 73*).

Which means that the Passion of the Church - like the Passion of Christ - has inexorably been set in motion. The mind of the persecutor is clear. The first shots have been fired. The global extent of the stakes show that the Catholic Church will for the first time in Her history be persecuted on a global scale. The Catholic Church, that is, which refuses to go along with the empire and church of Satan under whatever name. And in country after country, this Church will live forth in isolated Catholics-on-the-outer, living under unbearable pressure, political, economic, social and religious, to join up ...

And it is for the training of these Catholics that God gave us Vatican II ...

The testimonies and evidence are overwhelming.

Book I: Vatican II   71

- Our Lady speaks the Truth. And at Fatima She categorically declared that *"The good will be martyred."*

- The Bible speaks the Truth. And St. John categorically tells us that *"The whole world will run the after the beast, which will make war on the Saints and overcome them."*

- Pope St. Pius X speaks the truth when he informed us that the One-World 'Church' *"would bring back to the world the reign of legalised cunning, and brute force, and the oppression of the weak and of all those who toil and suffer."*

- Vatican II speaks the Truth. And in several places in its documents it reminded us of our duty *"to shed, if necessary, our blood for our friends and for Truth."*

- Finally, we can be sure that, ultimately, our enemies will speak the truth when they will say to us: *"Look, we wooed you, we ignored you, we warned you. You will not listen. Now we must 'wrathfully attack you' ..."*

These Catholics will be asked to completely join in the Mystical Life of Christ, which is a Life of self-immolation for the sins of the world. And so, the *means* and *inspiration* to join in the Mystical Life of Christ to such a degree lie hidden in the Mystery of the Church, which Herself draws strength continuously from this Mystical Life in Christ. This Life is **the** Mystery of the Church and can only be seen with the Supernatural Light and Eyes of Catholic Faith.

And if Vatican II, in the Providence of God, was meant to prepare Catholics in the process of being persecuted, for such a participation in the Mystery of the Church, then Vatican II itself must, to a very high degree, share in this Mystery, which means that it becomes incomprehensible in any other light except the strong Light of Catholic Faith. In this Light it did not matter which 'instruments' took part: the *Rhine* or the *Tiber*, but only what God created with these instruments for the Life of His chosen ones.

If people got confused after Vatican II, scandalized by Vatican II, or tried to manipulate Vatican II for their own designs and purposes: it all only showed the lack of Catholic Faith in these people, *their lack of oil ...*

- God knew that the persecuted Catholics during the most terrible persecutions yet to be unleashed, would feel alone, deserted, and would only have their Catholic Faith to guide them. So He made sure that in the training period immediately following on Vatican II, these conditions would be present to a lesser degree.

- He knew that during those persecutions His faithful ones would be requested to love their persecutors. So, in the training period, He provided us with innumerable opportunities to strengthen us in the exercise of this all-embracing demand.

- God remembered that in the Sacred Passion of His only-begotten Son, *ONLY OUR LADY* understood what was happening and what was requested of Her. So He made sure that Vatican II would once again reveal the most beautiful teaching on Our Lady and the Church for the consolation of all who would be prepared to stay with Her under the Cross.

- He also remembered how ill-prepared the Holy Apostles were when they came face to face with the disfigurement in His Son during His Sacred Passion. So He allowed a certain disfigurement in the Mystical Body of His Son in the post-Conciliar period, so that His persecuted faithful would draw strength for the time when the Catholic Church would follow Her Spouse *till the bitter end*.

And thus, in page after beautiful page, the Catholic Church poured out Her Love for humanity in the Second Vatican Council. The teilhardians, on their erroneous philosophy of *identity* and *sameness*, thought it was at last the signal they had been waiting for: to be finally allowed to *identify* themselves with the world and its ways on the evolutionary teachings of Teilhard de Chardin. And the Church let them go, knowing that much would be restored after Her own faithful would wash the whole world once again clean in their own blood.

<u>For further reading consult the following</u>:

- "Teilhard de Chardin and the Dutch Catechism";
- "The 'theology' of the Late Pierre Teilhard de Chardin S.J.".

[Editors comment. Both these books are included in *Selected Works Of Frits Albers Vol 1: Analysing The Errors And Exposing The Real Agenda Of Pierre Teilhard de Chardin S.J.* En Route Books and Media, 2024]

Dedicated, with great respect to the memory of Pope Paul VI, who literally lived Vatican II in the embrace of all who came to visit him, and who taught Vatican II in his everlasting encyclicals.

First Edition
On the Feast of the Holy Rosary,
Saturday, October 7th, 1978.
Second Edition
Holy Week, 1995.

Third Edition
February 2, 2000.

Fourth Edition
June 7, 2024

Postscript

Some thoughts on the document called "Vatican II"

The _purpose_ of this document is to show that, no matter what can be said about the turmoil surrounding the post-Conciliar Church, these upheavals cannot be laid at the doorstep of this unique Council. Just as the turmoil surrounding the passion and death of Our Blessed Lord on the first Good Friday could not be traced to the Son of God as the cause for this violent disruption. And just as the cause of the grave dislocation on that first Good Friday must be traced to the hatred deeply embedded in the false tradition of the Pharisees, priests and scribes at the end of the Old Dispensation, so it is that now the cause of the violence done to the Holy Church must be traced to the hatred the Modernists have for the Catholic Tradition of this unique Catholic Church; a hatred deeply embedded in their own false 'tradition'. And just as Our Blessed Lord on that first Good Friday allowed Himself to be sacrificed for the salvation of Jews and Gentiles, so was it that Vatican II allowed the Holy Church to be sacrificed for that same sinful humanity two thousand years later.

So, in **Chapter One** of this essay on Vatican II, the author takes a good, hard look at the pre-Vatican II scene, to see which section of the Catholic Church has the _right_ Catholic Tradition, and which section has the _wrong_, the _false_ 'tradition'. Furthermore, it is of great importance that readers of this document are under no illusion as to the _essence_ of the falsehood of this spurious 'tradition'.

Hence the in-depth treatment of this falsehood and of its world-wide spread and acceptance in the evolutionary 'philosophy' and 'theology' of the adherents of this modernist 'tradition'.

Chapter Two deals with the most important question of Catholicism in the modern world:

- which tradition presented at the gates of this genuine Council was allowed through, and
- which tradition was filtered out and rejected.

Tradition-with-a-capital-T, *Catholic Tradition,* was everywhere allowed through after suitable updating of matters of Catholic discipline, even in the documents where the Holy Church was breaking new ground.

Now it is indisputable that, if this Council came directly from the firm guidance of the Holy Spirit, the post-Conciliar turmoil around the changes in the Liturgy and around the two questions of "the genuine ecumenism" and "true religious liberty" could not possibly come from the Holy Spirit, could not possibly come from the Catholic Church, and so could not possibly come from Vatican II itself. Just as the upheavals around Our Lord's sacred Passion and Death could not possibly come from His teachings or from His sacred Person. The genuineness of Vatican II is found in the attentive reading of, and the prayerful meditation on its documents, as well as in the authority of the Holy See. Everything is up for grabs if the Council is rejected as an elaborate hoax, as a victory for the *Rhine,* that is for liberal Protestantism, which eventually must mean: for Modernism. Just as the crucifixion and death of Our

Lord must then be seen as a victory for His enemies, for Caiaphas and his mob. So the true meaning of Vatican II lies in its mystique. We have to tread very carefully here.

In **Chapter Three** we deal with the burning question: If Modernism, and with it the victory of its 'tradition' and 'inspiration', were ruthlessly filtered out of Catholicism by Vatican II, whence then the post-Conciliar turmoil?

This question is on a par with what we can ask ourselves with regard to the appearance of Our Lord and Saviour on earth, made real by the same firm guidance of the Holy Spirit at His Incarnation. If the Son of God had ruthlessly sifted out the falsehoods of the faked Jewish 'traditions' of His day from the Tradition He wished to leave as a legacy to His Church on earth, why then the utter confusion at the time of His sacred Passion and Death?

The answer is the same for both questions.

At the time of Christ it was allowed by God for the *Redemption* of a sinful human race, and 2000 years later, in our days, it is allowed by that same Divine Providence and Mercy for the application of this Redemption: the *Salvation* of that same sinful humanity. And just as Caiaphas' following had utterly resisted the acceptance of their defeat and the rejection for what they stood for at the hands of our Divine Saviour, but found a *bypass* around Him to hand Him over to Pilate for martyrdom, so it is with the Modernists of our days. They came into the sheep fold by some other means, and according to Our Lord's saying, they must be seen as brigands and robbers because they entered to maim and kill. The Jewish leaders of Our Lord's time wanted Him treated as an unmasked criminal, a hoax, and the Modernists of our own days, took control of local churches everywhere to do exactly the same with the Catholic Church. And just as with Christ before Pilate the Evangelist could write: *"And their cries gained the upper hand"* (Lk. 23:23), so it is in our days.

And so in this chapter 3 we deal with a question uppermost in our minds:

"What is driving these people? What is their motive? What is this fools gold so tantalising that they are prepared to stake everything on its acquisition, including their birthright to eternal life?" "What was driving Archbishop Marcel Lefèbvre into schism and to eventual excommunication?" The answers to these legitimate questions are clearly dealt with in this 3ʳᵈ chapter.

Chapter Four deals with the obvious question:

If the Modernists of our days succeeded in finding a bypass around Vatican II, were there any traces of this detour already in existence in the sense that, if there were, with whom did our enemies make common cause?

The changes in the *Liturgy* have been held up by innumerable Catholics as one cause for dissent. Others have pointed to the unfamiliar teaching of *the true ecumenism* and that on *true religious liberty*. Although the charity of Pope John Paul II has managed to find a way to keep many of these Catholics within the Catholic fold, individually they still have to answer before God how they see their inner dissent from Vatican II and the *Novus Ordo*. Just as the Jews outside Caiaphas' 'tradition' nevertheless had to answer for their doubts and misgivings with regard to Our Saviour's Passion and Death and His *Novus Ordo* of the New Sacrifice, insofar as they had allowed themselves to be guided and inspired by that 'tradition' at that most critical time of their lives. Although their modern counterparts are not the real enemies of Our Holy Mother the Catholic Church, they lose many graces attached to unreserved filial submission.

And so Chapter 4 deals with the plots and subversions of the real enemies, the Modernists and their interlaced networks, whereby they are connected with those outside the Church for Her destruction.

Finally, **Chapter Five** deals with the question of the *mystique* of Vatican II whereby it lives in the intimate union of the Spouse, the Mystical Body of Christ, with Her head, Christ. It was in the intimacy of this union that the Holy Catholic Church took Her most devoted children to the window opened by Pope John XXIII to see the plight of mankind as Christ saw it from His Cross. As is stated in this documentary, in several places of the documents of Vatican II, the faithful are not only reminded, but urged, to be prepared to shed their blood for the salvation of the world. And just as in Caiaphas' days his mob accelerated the Passion of Our Saviour Jesus Christ, so in our days the Modernists are doing exactly the same in regard to the Passion of Our Holy Mother the Catholic Church. From a vantage point such as this it has now become very clear indeed how much natural understanding and supernatural insights are missed by those who harbour and nurture in themselves misgivings and mistrust about any aspect of Vatican II.

In many countries of the world and their parishes the Novus Ordo is badly treated by priests who belong to, or are inspired by the Holy Church's enemies *in the bypass*. But so was the Sacred Body of Our Lord abused on the Friday after the Institution of the most Blessed Sacrament in the Cenacle. Unbearable for most except for Our Lady. We can go through the same mutilations at Her hand.

Book II

In Defense of the *Novus Ordo Missae* of His Holiness Pope Paul VI

Frits Albers, Ph.B.

First Edition, 1978
Second Edition, 2000
Third Edition, 2024

Introduction

In 1978 when the apologists of the suspended French Archbishop Marcel Lefèbvre and the promoters of the Latin Missal of Pope
St. Pius V (commonly known as the '*Tridentine Mass*') had moved
into top gear with the circulation of their material all around Australia, an ordered response did not come from the Australian Epis-
copal Conference, but was left to individual lay Catholics. The impact of the efforts of these apologists is largely neutralised by the
blatant and massive disobedience they advocate which does not
ride easily on Catholic shoulders. But their implantation of seeds of
doubt however insignificant in the beginning, necessitates the admission that an appeal to Catholic obedience is insufficient, since
doubt pertains to the realm of the intellect, of Faith, which happens
to be a different virtue from obedience. Doubt must be eradicated
with instruction in the Truth, with certainty and with Light, of
which the Catholic Church is the guardian.

Now, 22 years later, we witness a steady trickle of Australian
young men moving to the United States or to Europe to study at
"Una Voce" seminaries to be ordained exclusively in the Tridentine Rite with the resolute exclusion of saying any Mass in the
"*Novus Ordo Missae*" promulgated by His Holiness Pope Paul VI
as a result of the liturgical changes that had been introduced by the
Second Vatican Council.

Before one can hope to come to grips with the propaganda of
bodies such as "Una Voce" and Latin Mass agglomerates, and with
the suppression of Truth that is involved in such propaganda, it is

necessary to untangle the minds that produce and artificially prolong the "Una Voce" phenomenon.

As an introduction to the most serious charges that can be leveled at "Una Voce", we must first look at a few preliminary observations.

1. There is the absurd situation that by far the great majority that comprises the trickle mentioned above does not know Latin, and never has known the Latin Tridentine Mass. This means at least two things.

    (i) They cannot 'love' the Tridentine Mass, because no one can love what he does not know. They were '**talked into**' using exclusively the Tridentine Mass. Which means their motives for rejecting Vatican II and the "Novus Ordo Missae" do **not** come from love of Latin but from a totally different source. And

    (ii) In order to understand the contents of the Latin Mass of the Day, these young men are forced to go to an English translation in order that they can say the Latin parrot-fashion in the hope that some of the English meanings may stay with them during the Mass. This is ludicrous. They may as well say the Mass in English.

2. Our Blessed Lord faced the people of Jerusalem on His Cross on Calvary. He did not talk over His shoulder to tell His Mother "there is your son", or the repentant thief: "Today you will be with Me in Paradise". On Calvary He was the *Priest* as well as

the altar and the Victim, offering to God the Holy Sacrifice of the Mass. Likewise, in the Cenacle when He instituted the Blessed Eucharist in the mystical separation of His Body and Blood, He faced *as Priest* His disciples. For centuries afterwards, priests and bishops did the same.

3. The first Mass in the Cenacle was said in the vernacular. The language used was Aramaic. All the Masses the great St. Paul said were said in Greek, the same language used for ages in the lands surrounding the Mediterranean Sea. There is nothing wrong with a Mass said facing the people or saying it in the vernacular. One can only force the issue illegally and invalidly if one advances that Christ Himself was wrong.

4. Archbishop Cranmer had a mother, but that did not prevent him from tearing England away from the Holy Catholic Church. No doubt Luther had a mother who had great hopes of him. The same remark. If this is remote, the next one occurred in our own lifetime. Archbishop Lefebvre had a mother who no doubt was very proud of her son, but that did not prevent him causing a schism. Were all these mothers so mesmerised that they did not see the pitfalls their sons were heading for, taking millions with them?

We have now arrived at the most serious charges that can be leveled at "Una Voce". By way of an introduction I will quote here the last bit of the most recent email I received from a Una Voce woman from America. She first contacted me in March this year, (2000) but her thoughts were so tangled up that there was no hope of sorting her out. When she got back to me last week the situation had gone from bad to worse, much worse!

".... By the way, Archbishop Lefebvre asked a papal nuncio at Vatican II what had happened to the Kingship of Christ. That nuncio told him that it was no longer possible. The Archbishop had given his life working under the banner of Christ the King in Africa as a missionary. He was therefore rather shaken. The rejection of that papal teaching is why Catholic countries were ordered after the Second Vatican Council to abolish the old Catholic laws that upheld Christ's Kingship. That is why I asked, in abandoning this teaching, did the theologians at Vatican II in effect reduce doctrine to the level of speculative theory? If so, how can the Holy Ghost safe-guard a pastoral council if He isn't even safe-guarding doctrine?"

That this poor soul is utterly confused and has no idea what she is on about is putting it mildly. She fails to see that the question put by Archbishop Lefebvre to the anonymous nuncio is unsustained by evidence and so that the whole thing is nothing but hearsay. It is being used to force acceptance by all 'Catholics of goodwill' into what abyss Vatican II has sunk by the invincible action of the 'theologians', an insurmountable obstacle to the Holy Spirit. The speeches and writings of their more prominent leaders are full of that sort of rubbish. They clutch at that type of scurrilous prattle as if it gives some kind of reassurance to their rejection of Vatican II. Yet her open and all too candid admission of the blasphemy against the Holy Spirit contained in her last line goes unnoticed, showing clearly that this is openly bandied about by Una Voce and - going by the above letter - not only by the leadership of this bankrupt organisation but also by the membership. This means it must lie at the root of this movement. For years it was the stand taken up by the promoters of Archbishop Lefebvre who *did* know what they were doing in following the position of Archbishop Marcel Lefebvre.

If this blasphemy lies at the root of Una Voce as a whole, it must lie at the root of its individuals and so at the root of its 'ordinations'.

If questioned, some of these young candidates for the priesthood and the recently ordained priests themselves will of course deny that they have any problems either with Vatican II or the Novus Ordo or the Church and the Papacy who gave both of these to Catholics. With monotonous regularity (again, parrot-fashion) they will fall back on the Indult contained in Ecclesia Dei.

But no papal indult can cover up, let alone forgive, a sin of which Our Blessed Lord Himself has said that it will not be forgiven either in this life or in the next, especially if it is secretly nurtured in an individual to support the reason for a sustained rejection of the Decrees of an Ecumenical Council.

Thus Our Lord built in Sacred Scripture an insurmountable obstacle to this kind of dead faith and its supercilious, parrot-fashion expression for the protection of His faithful children. It is contained in the Letter of St. James ch. 2. But first an introductory line.

Like the Modernists, the Una Voce crowd also found a bypass around Vatican II which allows them to ignore that great Council with impunity, so they think.

This leads to the crux of the matter.

To explain what I am driving at, I have to go to the Letter of St. James.

St. James wrote:

"This is the way to talk to people of that kind (who say they have faith but no good works to show for it): You say you have faith and I have good deeds. I show to you that I have faith by showing you my good deeds; now you prove to me that you have faith without any good deeds to show."

So I say to these Una Voce priests:

I can show you that I have Faith by showing you my good works in relation to Vatican II, the Novus Ordo and the Papacy that gave all this to the Church. I wrote in defence of Vatican II many times. I go daily to a Novus Ordo Mass and have written extensively in defence of the Novus Ordo and the Popes that gave all this to us. In 1974 I have begged a fine Priest on his deathbed not to die at variance with Pope Paul VI over the Novus Ordo. I have never been found wanting in these practices.

Now you show me that you have faith in Vatican II, in the *Novus Ordo Missae* and in the Popes who imposed Vatican II and the Novus Ordo on the whole Church by even one good deed in direct relation to those three. You show me by even one good work that you accept Vatican II in toto, that you accept its changes in the liturgy (Novus Ordo) and that you accept the Pontiffs who imposed those two on us. Do not come and tell me that you have an Indult: my fight is **not** with the Latin Mass but with your good works or the absence of them in support or non-support of your faith. If you cannot quote even a single good work in support of Vatican II or the Novus Ordo, then I quote to you St. James again:

"Do realise, you senseless man, that faith without good works is DEAD!"

Without even a single good work to show, a Catholic's faith in Vatican II, in the Novus Ordo, is *dead*. It doesn't exist. Your exclusive 'faith' in a papal indult will *never* revive a dead faith without good works. Will never forgive a doubt about the Holy Spirit. For the life of me I cannot even begin to envisage that God would call anyone to a dead-end 'faith'. That God would call anyone to a priesthood at the root of which is found a dead faith. The upshot is then that you, young men, gave yourself a vocation. That you worked your own way up to the priesthood if you were not called by God. Your name may have been called by the bishop, but if you have no faith in Vatican II or in the Novus Ordo, or in the Popes who gave all that incredibly rich material to the Church, you were not called by God.

The whole Latin Mass movement has no substance. For that reason the Holy Father did not think the issue important enough to risk the loss of one's eternity on it. So he hauled them back on board by giving in to their demand. Otherwise many of them would not have come. But that does not mean that, if at the root of these people's internal forum there still lies a disbelief or a doubt about the power of the Holy Spirit to guide an Ecumenical Council to its foolproof end, then this hauling back on the Barque of St. Peter does **not** cover or forgive this individual sin. The Tridentine Mass can only be said safely and validly

(a) if by their good works these priests show to the satisfaction of St. James and the whole Church that they have a lively Faith in all the Decrees of Vatican II and accept unreservedly the Novus Ordo as coming from the bosom of the Church, and

(b) have received sacramental forgiveness for any blasphemy of the Holy Spirit in relation to these three vital points. Otherwise this blasphemy will be a severe impediment to the validity of any ordination.

The 1978 Australian Scene

When in 1969 *Pope Paul VI* gave to the Catholic Church the *Novus Ordo Missae* with his Bull *Missale Romanum*, he implemented the changes in the Liturgy requested by the Second Vatican Council. As with all things new: the changes were not immediately understood, and so they received a mixed reception.

One of the results of the change was the necessity to set aside Papal Bulls which had laid down rules for the Church's liturgy up till then The most important one of these was the bull *Quo Primum*, by which his holiness Pope St. Pius V, in 1570, had codified the Mass liturgy for the Western Church, as requested by the Council of Trent. At that time, the Liturgy of the Catholic Church was by no means uniform; and we must not forget, that the 40 Holy Martyrs did not die for what became known as the *Tridentine Rite*, but for the old *Sarum Rite* of liturgy, which at that time was used in England.

One of the earliest reactions against *Missale Romanum* and the *Novus Ordo* it introduced, was the opinion that the bull *Quo Primum* of Pope St. Pius V, by which the Sarum Mass was derogated to be followed by the Tridentine Rite, could not be set aside. This means that we do not need much imagination to realise that some of the relatives and friends of the 40 Holy Martyrs could quite well have had the same feelings towards Pope St. Pius V for suppressing the very Mass format for which the Forty had given their lives as are now being directed towards Pope Paul VI for having derogated the Tridentine Rite.

May, therefore, these glorious Martyrs sustain all of us who at the present moment have difficulty accepting Pope Paul VI's decision, as no doubt they helped their own contemporaries to accept the verdict of Pope St. Pius V.

For people who have kept a close watch on the beginnings of this movement, it is not difficult to supply this certainty and instruction. It is for this reason that I have accepted an invitation by the President of the *John XXIII Fellowship* to write a more detailed refutation of the claims and statements made by the Tridentine Mass promoters, especially in their recently circulated material. Their statements and claims cover four very clearly distinct areas:

➢ History,
➢ Tradition,
➢ Theology (under which I include Canon Law and Scripture),
➢ and finally Catholic Faith.

In each of these areas the 'Tridentiners' (for short) use faulty and gravely erroneous argumentation which I will endeavour to bring out, to be followed by what I consider, and the experts I consulted with me, to be the correct teaching.

Finally, before we will have a closer look at their faulty arguments from *History*, it will be instructive to familiarise ourselves with the very early beginnings of this movement. This will help us to resist the temptation of becoming over-awed by the avalanche of material they have produced to substantiate their case.

That initially the Latin Mass Movement did not directly dispute the authority of Pope Paul VI, nor objected to the *Novus Ordo* itself, is made abundantly clear to anyone who reads the account of events from which all members of this movement take their cue and their lead:

> ➢ the articles by Père Dulac in *Itineraires* 1970, from No. 139 onwards,
> ➢ and the Conference of Abbé Georges de Nantes at Nancy, June 19, 1970, *Contre-Réformation Catholique*, (CRC), June 1970.

There is no escape: no matter how hard they tried in subsequent years to make it appear that the inner force of the movement is based on internal criticism of the *Novus Ordo* and of Vatican II, followed by serious attacks on the Holy Father and the Vatican itself: historically it is beyond dispute that the whole movement is based on one thing and one thing only: their totally mistaken idea that the bull *Quo Primum* of Pope St. Pius V could not be set aside by Pope Paul VI. This mistake is the sole basis of the earliest origin of the whole controversy. Therefore, for a start of our rebuttal, it is sufficient to know that the earliest article of Abbé de Nantes: "*Forbidding the Holy Roman Mass*" (CRC June 1970) deals primarily with the question of the inviolability of *Quo Primum* and related matters. Even if in later developments much weight was attached to the theological criticism of Card. Ottaviani, in this earliest article the 'Ottaviani Intervention' only received no more than a brief mention. So sure were the earliest critics of Pope Paul VI that the whole question hinged around the inviolability of *"Quo Primum"*. It was a sad day for the modern Church that, when they became aware of their mistake, these people persisted in their rebellion, showing conclusively that far more was involved than the question of a new liturgy, a new Mass format.

Argument From History

There is a proper way and a misleading way to bring out facts from history to prove one's case. The 'Tridentiners' make much use of historical facts to show the strength of their resistance, but the validity of this resistance receives its first severe set-back if it can be shown that their argumentation from history is faulty. Let us analyse some of the facts they bring up.

1. The present Holy Father could not set aside the Bull *Quo Primum*.

   This is historically untenable, but since this question cannot be satisfactorily dealt with from a purely historical approach, since it touches on Catholic Faith, it is better left for consideration till the next Section under the heading *"Argument from Tradition"*.

2. "The change in the words of the Consecration of the wine renders the Consecration invalid or at least so doubtful as to be forbidden".

   This too could be refuted from a proper historical consideration, but since this question also touches on Catholic Faith it is better left until the next Section which deals with Catholic Tradition.

3. It is a fact of history that over the centuries many Canons (Eucharistic Prayers) have been used and are still in use, and that there exists a great variety of words of the Consecration. One of the finest scholars in Europe at that time, the redoubtable Fr. Prof. Dr. J. van der Ploeg, O.P. of Nijmegen, Holland, has a list of dozens of different words of the Consecration, which have been used at one time or another in the Church's long history, and would, if used today, still validly consecrate. They all agree on the <u>one essential</u>: the words 'This is My Body' and 'This is My Blood', or 'This is the chalice of My Blood'. These words constitute the words of the Consecration, the form of the Sacrament. If these words are spoken by any validly ordained Priest anywhere in the world over the proper matter, bread and wine, Transubstantiation takes place.

4. It is another fact of history that any Pope at any time may ask anybody his or her opinion on any matter, particularly so, if these men and women are recognised scholars in their own field. Pope Paul did **not** need the approval of the various Latin Mass Associations to ask scholars in Ancient Church History their opinion, if a particular Canon was used in the 3rd or the 4th Century. To say, in this context, that the *Novus Ordo* was composed 'with the aid of 6 non-Catholics' is so blatantly mischievous as to be wholly malicious. It does not matter a tinker who looks on when the Holy Father does something (observers) nor whom the Holy Father asks for his opinion. Once, after all has been said and done, the Holy Father says: "And now, this is it", the matter is settled, raised from the profane to the sacred;

and no one can from then on say: "There goes 20% of my opinion", or "50% of yours". Never did the Holy Father ask any of those 6 observers: "Is this change Protestant enough to your liking?"

5. Many derailments in the long history of the Church have been brought about, because the wrong effects have been linked to the wrong historical causes, mostly because superficial thinkers have used over-simplification. The one fact that there are upheavals in the Church today: apostasy, heresy preaching, defections, and also the other fact that we had an Ecumenical Council, gives no one the right to link these two as cause and effect. The same goes for the linking of the upheavals with the *Novus Ordo*. The Latin Mass people relish in the simplistic logic: there are many bad things in the Church and we also had a change in the Mass format. Therefore, the change in the Mass format must have been a bad one, because the bad things in the Church followed from it. This sort of "logic", or circular argument, is used extensively by the followers of spurious 'apparitions':

(a) someone claims to have had apparitions from Our Lady, telling him/her that things are bad and that there are bad bishops. (b) The bishop(s) investigating these reports, eventually declare(s) that these 'apparitions' and 'messages' lack any supernatural origin. (c) The seers then turn around and say: These messages are true, because they stated that bad bishops would ban them. This bishop bans them, so he must be bad, and the apparition was true. {That this is not a frivolous example is borne out by the fact that, especially roundabout 1972, priests in letters to their bishops informing them of their decision of no longer saying the *Novus Ordo* Mass, appealed to these 'apparitions' in support of their disobedience}. But neither the Holy Father nor the *Novus Ordo* may be declared bad just because there are abuses in the Church. For if the Holy Father happens to be a saint in reality, and if the *Novus Ordo* proves in reality to be the continuation of the Perpetual Sacrifice of the New Covenant, then the evils in the Church must have other causes, which of course they have. The worth of the Holy Father and the nature of the *"Novus Ordo* are to be established on their own proper evidence before anything can be linked with them in a cause-effect relationship. Both history and logic demand scrupulous adherence to this.

6. Finally, the 'Tridentiners' suppress historical facts which would neutralise their arguments. For example,

(a) Pope Paul VI is not the first Pope in history who made changes to the 'immutable code' of his predecessors; he is not even the first Pope who made changes to the bull *Quo Primum"*. (See the next Section).

(b) Cardinal Ottaviani made a genuine declaration of acceptance of the *Novus Ordo*. [See *Newsletter* of the International Catholic Priests Association., Vol. VI, No.1, p. 44, where the author of "A Criticism of 'Changes in the Mass'" (a book by Michael Davies) quotes the authority of Archbishop Robert Dwyer, 1976].

(c) There is unquestionable historicity of the Canons in use (except the 4th one).

(d) Twice by letters written in his own handwriting, the Holy Father has disclaimed all rumours 'that he is a captive', 'that he is drugged', 'that he would be a plastic pope', etc. From these letters by the Holy Pontiff to Archbishop Marcel Lefèbvre, it has become a fact of history that the Holy Father affirms with all the authority of the Supreme Pontiff, that the measures promulgated by him in application of the Decrees of Vatican II in the sphere of liturgy and discipline, must be considered as being of a doctrinal character and thus that the living Magisterium of the Church is intimately involved in this whole matter. To reject the New Mass Liturgy - as Archbishop Lefèbvre does - is to call into question not only the authoritative teaching of the Church, but also the work of the Holy Spirit in preserving a genuine Council of the whole Church against error and human interference. These are essentially matters of Faith. It is for this reason that a much better case can be made against the 'Tridentiners' with an *Argumentation from Tradition*, which will be considered now.

Argument From Tradition

Tradition in the Catholic Church differs from ordinary human history in that Catholics believe that Tradition, although part of human history, nevertheless is also part of Revelation, and therefore falls under the special protection that God has attached to the authentic preservation of His Revelation to men. Tradition is a sure guide of how Revelation is to be lived. It is called 'Tradition' precisely because the full title in Latin is "Traditio Revelationis": the handing over of Revelation, i.e. the Deposit of Faith, from each generation to the next one. We have God's guarantee that Tradition, taken in this sense, is also infallibly protected against the handing over of heresy and error. And if heresy and error are being passed on from one generation to the next, then we have God's guarantee that, even if this is done *by* Catholics, it is never done validly in Name of the Catholic Church, but outside Her and away from Her. And so we have the historical fact that, even if the Catholic Church will never preach nor embrace heresy and error as part of God's Revelation, individual Catholics, even large groups of Catholics, have from time to time succumbed to both.

Since heresy and falsehood are contradictions of Truth, especially Revealed Truth, they pertain primarily to the intellect, to one's faith and beliefs. That's why there is much greater freedom and liberty in the Church in practices, and discipline, ways of expressing the same Faith. Therefore, although a change in practice, in discipline, does not automatically reflect a change in Faith and belief, nevertheless it is absolutely true that a change in Faith will eventually express itself in a change in practice. Removing the statue of Our Lady from a church does not necessarily, in itself, reveal a loss of Faith in Our Lady, but a loss of Faith in Our Lady will eventually result in the removal of Her statues.

The government of the Church is vested in Her Head, which on earth is the Pope who is primarily protected by God from heresy preaching. And it is precisely in this whole area surrounding the person of the Holy Father, that we have to look for the greatest trouble the Tridentine Mass followers have brought upon themselves. For that reason it is important to keep their earliest beginnings in perspective. Initially it may have seemed that they only differed from the Pope in a simple matter of practice, of Church discipline, from which it was not immediately evident if this also involved a change of Faith. But over the years it has become more and more apparent that initially a change of Faith *was present* from which it became inevitable that a change in practice would follow. For if their original difficulty with *Missale Romanum* v *Quo Primum* had been adequately solved for them (which as we will see is not hard to do), one would expect them to be relieved and readily accept the *Novus Ordo*. But this has not been the case. This makes one wonder if the *Novus Ordo* really is the point in dispute. Driven further and further into the revelation of the real issue, it came finally to light that the kernel of the whole revolt is the acceptance of Vatican II and of his Holiness Pope Paul VI as the legitimate Pope. In other words: if the Mass format had not changed, these people, from their hidden change-of-faith, would have found some other excuse to differ from the Holy Father sufficiently to go their own way away from the teachings of Vatican II.

Let us now follow their argumentation from Tradition to see if this conclusion is valid.

1. The very first stand taken by the 'Tridentiners' was, that the Bull *Quo Primum* of Pope St. Pius V could never be set aside. According to the pamphlets circulated around Australia in the late seventies, they are still of that opinion, i.e. when dealing with (so

they think) ignorant people. Since they base their belief in the immutable character of *Quo Primum* on the very wording of the Bull, it should be sufficient to show from Tradition that Papal Bulls, using exactly the same phraseology, have been set aside by subsequent Popes, if the Bulls dealt with matters of Church discipline.

(a) My first example refers to the 'emphatically strong condemnation' that the same Pope St. Pius V uttered against anyone who would dare to change or modify the Roman Breviary, promulgated by the Bull *Quod a nobis* of June 7th, 1568. Like the wording of *Quo Primum*, any interference with the new breviary would likewise bring about the indignation of Almighty God and the wrath of the Apostles Peter and Paul. Yet 34 years later (1602) Pope Clement VIII, and again 29 years later (1631) Pope Urban VII introduced new changes, *and each of these two Popes ended their bulls with the same solemn declaration.* The whole pseudo-argument of the 'Tridentiners' evaporates even further if one considers that a Pope *and Saint,* Pope St. Pius X, did not consider himself bound by the disciplinary Bulls of his predecessors, and with his own Bull *Divino Afflatu* of 1911 issued his radically reformed Roman Breviary, and ended once again with a repetition of all the strong words used by St. Pius V. Yet again, Pope Paul VI, on the 1st of November 1970, issued his *Liturgia Horarum* in conformity with the directives put forward by the Second Vatican Council.

(b) Here is a second example. On June 23, 1773, Pope Clement XIV suppressed the Jesuit Order through his Brief *Dominus ac Redemptor*. The language of this Apostolic Writ once again declares 'the perpetual validity of the decision then taken', 'to be inviolately observed for future times'. Yet, in 1814 Pope Pius VII re-established the Society of Jesus.

(c) Finally, to show that no Pontiff is restricted by the untouchable edicts of his predecessors and - what is more - to show that His Holiness Pope Paul VI was not the first Pope in history to make changes to the Liturgy covered by *Quo Primum*, it is well known that Pope Pius XII reorganised the Liturgy of the Holy Week and re-introduced. the Paschal Vigil, infringing, with these changes on *Quo Primum*.

2. The next move by the 'Latin Mass Associations' was to 'prove' that, even if theoretically the Bull *Quo Primum* could be set aside by a future Pope, that this was nevertheless not done by the Bull *Missale Romanum* of Pope Paul VI. Either - some claim - because Pope Paul VI had no intention of abrogating *Quo Primum* or - others claim - his Bull *Missale Romanum* is null and void. And so - they all claim - *Quo Primum* still stands and must be adhered to.

As a back-stop for their first argument it is even weaker and more fallacious than their first one. That the Holy Father intended to replace the previously existing Liturgy, there can be no doubt whatsoever. His very words (AAS, vol. 61, 1969, p. 217-222) could not be clearer:

"We intend that the Statutes and Prescriptions which We have established shall remain firm and efficacious, both in the present and in the future, notwithstanding those Constitutions and Apostolic Ordinances of our Predecessors, including those which require special mention before they could be derogated."

Canon 22 of the (then) Codex of Canon Law supports the claim that *Missale Romanum*; has superseded *Quo Primum*:

"A subsequent Law abrogates a previous one, if, made by competent Authority, it **re-organises** the whole matter of the previous legislation."

The legislation of Pope Paul VI did not do away with the Mass: it merely reorganised the Liturgy.

In order to sustain their claim 'that *Missale Romanum* of Pope Paul is null and void', the 'Tridentiners' now have to prove that Canon Law assumed incorrectly 'that Pope Paul VI is competent authority'. But then we have strayed far away from the *Novus Ordo* and have arrived at the heart of the revolt of the Latin Massers: their open claim 'that Pope Paul is an illegitimate Pope because he is - and was - a heretic.' (See the various "Newsletters" so-called of the Latin Mass Society of Australia). But if this lies at the bottom of the Latin Massers' case, then their case is built on an absurdity. In the final Section, when we will let the Light of Catholic Faith shine on this whole matter, we will pick up this question again and will deal with it further.

3. A third concentrated attack from the 'Tridentiners' which is better settled from Tradition rather than from theology (the next Section) is their assertion that the change in the words of the

Consecration of the wine renders the Consecration (i) invalid
(some), or (ii) gravely doubtful (others) and so, on whatever
count (iii) to be avoided at all cost (all). This is a more serious
charge and calculated to cause some anxiety amongst fair-
minded priests and lay-people. If the point is raised in the absence of charge, mistrust and invective, an answer can be found
dealing with the discrepancy between the Latin *Missa Normativa* (i.e. the *Novus Ordo* in Latin) and the various translations.
But for this it is necessary that people are genuinely interested in
an answer and are not subscribing to other charges and claims
made by the Latin Mass people and refuted elsewhere. In other
words, we can only settle this question completely satisfactorily,
if we accept Pope Paul as the legitimate Holy Father competent
to introduce the *Novus Ordo Missae*, which we accept as coming
from his will. In this climate of trust and Faith the difficulty still
exists, but an answer is not impossible.

a. A first answer is that no theologian holds (since it was nev-
    er taught by the Church) that only the words of the Conse-
    cration as laid down by the Bull *Quo Primum* constitute the
    form of the Sacrament of the Blessed Eucharist. As already
    stated above, there are so many different forms of the
    words of the Consecration, at one time or another used by
    the Church, that the general consensus is that the proper
    form of the Sacrament of the Blessed Eucharist is:

    "*This is My Body*" and "*This is (the chalice of) My Blood*",
    spoken over the proper *matter*: bread and wine.

This takes the sting out of the argument that the English words of the Consecration of the wine make the Consecration invalid or even doubtful, since the remaining words are spoken *after* Transubstantiation has taken place.

b. A second answer must settle the question:

"Is it true that a lie has been introduced in the very heart of Catholicism, the Holy Sacrifice of the Mass, by the change of 'pro multis' in the Latin *Novus Ordo* to the 'for all' in the vernacular?"

    i.   The beginning of the answer is that, apart from the words already mentioned, "*This is My Body*" and "*This is My Blood*", we do not know the exact words Christ used after that. "*For many*" is used in Mt. 24:28 and Mk 14:24, but not in Luke or St. Paul. St. Luke says "*pro vobis*" "for you" (plural). How restrictive is that? If the Apostles were the representatives of the whole human race, the meaning '*for all*' as '*for you all*' is then quite legitimate. For Christ *did* shed His Blood 'for all men'.

    ii. St. Paul is emphatic that Christ died for the whole human race. See e.g. Rom. 8:32, 2 Cor. 5:14, Rom. 5:12 sqq., 1 Tim. 2:6, 9:10, to mention only a few passages. See also Jn. 1:29, 3:16, 17, 6:33, 51, 1 Jn 2:2, 4:14, etc. All these texts make it perfectly clear that there is no heresy on the lips of a priest when he says during the Consecration: "*This is the cup of My Blood...which is shed for you and for all so that sins may be forgiven*". The change in words reflects the classical distinction between the *subjective* and *objective* Redemption won by Christ, i.e. between 'salvation' (many) and 'redemption' (offered to all).

iii. Finally, may I refer the reader (and I do hope that they will bring the following to the notice of any 'Tridentiner' in their circle of friends) to quite a few 'Prayers over the Gifts' immediately before the Preface and the beginning of the Eucharistic Prayer *in the old Tridentine Mass prescribed by Pope St. Pius V*, 'Several Prayers for the Dead':

"Grant us we beseech Thee O Lord, that this offering may benefit the soul of Your servant Bishop N, since through the offering of these gifts *You grant that the sins of the whole world are loosened*'.

"Annue nobis, quaesumus Domine, ut animae famuli tui N. Episcopi haec prosit oblatio, quam immolando *totius mundi tribuisti relaxari derelicta*".

This is much stronger than the words of the English Consecration and should, to be consistent, be open to doubt to anyone who doubts the words of the (English) Consecration without due regard for papal authority and Church Tradition.

Christ not only shed His Blood *"for all"* (St. Paul, St. John): according to this 'Prayer over the Gifts', the renewal of His Sacrifice in every Mass is for the *undoing* (relaxari) of <u>the sins of the whole world</u>. In the old Tridentine Rite these words constituted the heart of Christ's Sacrifice, both on Calvary and in every Mass as the re-enactment of this Sacrifice, and they were pronounced very close to the centre of every Mass: the Consecration. They never meant, or stated, that *all men* would be saved. Neither, therefore, should this exclusive meaning be attached to these words when they are in use in the New Rite. The old Tridentine Rite was not frightened to stress the universality of Christ's Sacrifice on the Cross and in the Mass. Neither, therefore, should we.

More can be said about this very question, but this is as far as it can be taken from Tradition. In the next two sections, Theology and Faith, we will come back to it for further development. Suffice to say here that there are words of the Consecration which do not include 'pro multis', 'for many', showing that these words are *not* part of the *form* of the Sacrament.

Argument From Theology

In dealing with questions of theology it must be remembered that theology is not Faith. A ton of theology will not by itself produce a grain of Faith. Faith in the Catholic Church is a Supernatural, Infused, Divine Gift from God. Theology is human reasoning about God's Gifts to man: Revelation. And so all it can do is to supply sincere people with good reasons to believe and to give support to the foundations of our Faith. Good theology makes one grateful to God for a growing understanding of one's Faith. Theology depends very much on Catholic Faith. Without it, it degenerates very rapidly into humanism, getting lost in social engineering. But Faith does not depend on theology, but on prayer and penance and many (heroic) acts of Faith.

What do we see happen, when 'theology' falls into the hands of the 'Tridentiners'? We see it used for the exact opposite: not to support Catholic Faith in the Catholic Church, in the Papacy and in the Catholic Mass; but to twist that Faith in support of self-interest: to make good Catholics doubt, and to make them follow private erratic opinions and interpretations. Theology was never meant for that, and for that very reason we should not be surprised that in the long bursts of invectives used by these dissidents, we find no theology and hardly - if any - honesty. Whoever wrote *The Ottaviani Intervention* wrote 27 falsehoods which will give him precious little for his trouble. With the best possible will in the world it is absolutely impossible to fit any reasoned theology into that diatribe. The effort was meant to inflame the passions and emotions.

- The *Letter to the Bishops* contains the same sweeping exaggerations by which the followers of Archbishop Marcel Lefèbvre have made themselves notorious.
- The third pamphlet distributed around Australia, denying Pope Paul VI the right and the competence to set aside the Tridentine Missal, is wrong in principal, and so no 'theology' so-called can rectify that. As we saw, Pope Paul VI had

both the wish and the competence to set aside *Quo Primum* and he is supported here by Tradition and Canon Law.

- Which leaves us with the last pamphlet: *Catholics, ask Questions!* The thing is so obviously partisan that the authors have allowed themselves to be carried away by their own propaganda, and in their indignation have completely forgotten the title. Instead of allowing us to ask questions, *we are told* statement after statement about which it is impossible to ask any questions, let alone theological questions ...

Take, for example, their very first statement, meant to arouse our burning indignation, which would blind us so much that we forget to ask questions about it; but instead, would hopefully induce us to tell as many other Catholics as possible: '*The new order of the Mass was composed with the active cooperation of six Protestant clergymen*'.

This is a deliberate lie, calculated to do untold damage to Catholic minds.

Amongst the scores of Catholic scholars we find five or six Protestant observers, some of whom were recognised scholars in their own field. The Holy Father <u>never ever</u> asked them: '*Is this change protestant enough to your liking?*' Instead, questions like these may have been put to them: '*Tell us from your own expertise, was this part of the liturgy used in the time of St. Ambrose, or in the time of St. Hyppolite?*' At least Michael Davies in his book *Changes in the Mass* has the belated decency to include at the end a brief note that Archbishop *Bugnini* categorically denies such conniv-

ance. But then, what is left over of the reputation of this Archbishop after the 'Tridentiners' went to town on him. As we will see in
the final Section of this paper: to give to the whole Church a re-
vised Missal about one of the Sacraments involves papal infallibility, since it directly touches on *Catholic Faith* in a Sacrament.
Therefore the miserable blowing-up-out-of-all-proportion of "Six
Protestant Ministers taking over the Vatican to devise a 'Protestant
Mass'" is such a ludicrous red herring as to become wholly malicious and mischievous. Thank God the Holy Father had the fore-
sight, under the direct guidance of the Holy Spirit, to ask these men
along if only to show up the unbelievable pettiness of the fully-
blown 'Tridentiners'.

The only semblance of an attempt at some real theology is
found on pp. 5-8 in this circular where it tries vainly to come to
grips with the change in the words of the Consecration of the wine
from the Missa Normativa (or the Latin *Novus Ordo*) into various
languages. This has already been dealt with more appropriately in
the previous Section on Tradition, but I will review here with the
use of some comments what the authors have to say on this. I
quote:

"At the Last Supper Our Lord said that His Blood would be shed
<u>for you and for many</u>...." (my stress).

None of the Gospels and none of the Letters of St. Paul combine
together the words "for you" and "for many". As we saw, it is not
clear which exact words Our Lord used at the institution of the
Blessed Eucharist in addition to the ones necessary for the *'form'* of
the Sacrament: "This is My Body" and "This is (the chalice of) My
Blood". In the Gospels of St. Matthew and St. Mark He is quoted

as having said *"for many"*. In St. Luke's Gospel He is quoted as having said *"for you"*. (See for more detail the previous Section, Argument From Tradition).

St. Paul writes in 1 Cor. 11:23 sqq., quoting Our Lord as having said to him,

"<u>For this is what I received from the Lord</u> and in turn passed on to you, that in the same night that He was betrayed the Lord Jesus … took the cup after supper and said: '<u>This cup is the New Covenant in My Blood</u>. Whenever you drink it, do this as a memorial of Me'."

There are **no** additional words added to the *form* of the Sacrament, that is, to the words necessary to confect the Transubstantiation of the wine. No *"for all"*, no *"pro multis"*, no *"pro vobis"*. It is impossible to either maintain or to accept that St. Paul received a lie from Our Lord.

I quote again:

"The words '<u>for all men</u>' are not found in any bible …"

This is an obvious falsehood. I have already indicated some of the many passages in the New Testament where the doctrine of the universality of Christ's Sacrifice, the shedding of His Precious Blood, is taught to us as a Revealed Truth, or Catholic Dogma.

"…or in any Christian liturgy anywhere".

This again is a falsehood. As I have already shown previously: it is clearly taught in the Liturgy of Pope St. Pius V, where it is not only taught by approved prayers and lessons 'that Christ shed His Blood once for all men', but where it is also clearly taught that the Sacrifice of the Mass itself is also offered to God for the forgiveness of the sins of the whole world. This dogma is denied by the 'Tridentiners'. They hold that the Sacrifice of the Mass is *only* offered to God for the *many* who avail themselves of its fruits. So it was very timely that the Holy Father Pope Paul VI approved of means that would bring this frightful misconception to the surface, in order that it could be effectively dealt with. Every time the 'Tridentiners' hear the words *"for all men"* they get the jitters like the old Jansenists whose heresies and misconceptions they have taken over. They deliberately and obstinately keep on 'preaching' to others what they believe themselves: that the words *'for all men'* must always and everywhere mean only one thing: that all men are saved. Even if they reluctantly admit that it may be true in theory that Christ shed His Blood on Calvary for all men, they are adamant in their belief and teaching that the Sacrifice of the Mass is only offered for those who avail themselves of its fruits.

Well, with all due respect, but that would then exclude themselves.

Since the remaining of this pamphlet is only a boring repetition of the words *'forgery'*, *'sacrilege'*, *'lies'* and the usual diatribe against the Church and the person of the Holy Father, I will leave it at that. The Holy Father uses *'per tutti'*, *'for all'* when he says Mass in Italian.

Argument From Faith

In dealing with hard-core 'Tridentiners', why is it so impossible to get through to them? Why do the reasoned arguments of Catholics from History, Theology, even Tradition, have no effect on them? Because, in final analysis, when all human arguments are exhausted and no longer anything else can be brought out to be held up to them, it is a question of Faith, *Catholic Faith*. A Light so powerful that, without it, arguments from other sources *which depend on that Light*, cannot produce the desired results on their own. With their changed faith the 'Tridentiners' have, in various degrees, separated themselves from the Holy Father with a real danger of becoming modern schismatics. What started off as a small disagreement has grown into a deep-seated split involving much more than a new Mass.

Thus it should not come as a surprise to Catholics that the most potent argumentation that can be brought out in favour of the *Novus Ordo* is the one from Catholic Faith. The 'Tridentiners' will heartily agree that it is a matter of Faith, and so it has now become a matter of great importance to decide which side kept the Catholic Faith.

(1) The first serious error of the 'Tridentiners' to be dealt with, which directly pertains to Catholic Faith, states that 'the new Mass does not involve infallibility'. Fr. James Wathen OSJ wrote this in his book *The Great Sacrilege* (TAN books, Rockford, Illinois, USA), dealing with it in a completely erroneous manner. The fraud is repeated in *Catholics, ask questions!*, circularised around Australia in the late seventies (p. 4-5). Printed there for all to read is this complete reversal of Catholic teaching:

"In 1969 the new order of the Mass was condemned on 27 counts by Cardinals Ottaviani and Bacci and other Catholic theologians as being unacceptable as a Catholic Mass.... So this Mass has been conclusively shown (sic!) by theologians to be not the

Catholic Mass we used to have. Did you know that? You would think that the Church authorities would be grateful for this weighty judgment ... Yet Pope Paul ignored this authoritative verdict that the new Mass was not a true Catholic Mass and imposed the new Mass on the Catholic Church".

We can at least be grateful that we are not told here that it was Archbishop Bugnini who gave us the *Novus Ordo*. It is clearly shown here that they know *where the new Mass came from*. The authors continue:

"Are we now to believe that the 'approval' of a Pope can change heresy into orthodoxy, can turn a non-Mass into a Mass?"

This is then followed by some '*ex cathedra*' statement from these followers of Archbishop Lefèbvre in which these 'Tridentine popes' take it upon themselves to continue their erroneous beginnings with an appeal to and their explanation of 'papal infallibility' used against Pope Paul VI (see 2.). To be concluded by the classical 'anathema-in-reverse':

"He does not help a mistaken Pope who aids and abets his error".

As said, this is a complete reversal of Faith which was **not** followed by as formidable a Catholic as was Cardinal Ottaviani. Why?

Because this great scholar did not condemn the new Mass 'on 27 counts'. We know that he wrote a few thoughtful observations which then got bracketed with the garbage that was concocted by lesser luminaries to be presented to the world as *the Ottaviani intervention*. We also know that this great man submitted his own judgment to the superior authority of Pope Paul. Again: Why? Because this unique scholar and true theologian knows *the correct procedure*: true theology and true theologians fall silent when the Holy Father officially declares <u>what belongs to the *form* of a Sacrament</u>, since there he is infallible. What belongs to the *form* of a Sacrament *must* be accepted by Catholic Faith and in that a Pope *cannot err*. This is so universally accepted that the 'Tridentiners' simply <u>had</u> to go further and declare Pope Paul himself illegal and an anti-pope. Instead of the Holy Father 'falling silent' in the face of weighty arguments, as these 'Tridentiners' demand with their colossal impudence, weighty arguments evaporate in the presence of papal teaching. The *Novus Ordo* has an Offertory, a Consecration and a Communion, the three essentials of a Catholic Mass, guaranteed under papal infallibility.

But once again (and now taken to its ultimate perspective, Catholic Faith): what about the '*lie*' introduced in the words of the Consecration of the wine?

Just as the Catholic Church at the time of the Council of Trent had the unquestionable power to take the words of Christ from two different places of the New Testament and put them together in the Consecration, so has the Church of our time, the time of Vatican II, the same power to do exactly the same. In 1570 the Church took words from St. Matthew and St. Luke and put them together. And now, guided by the same Holy Spirit, the same Church takes actual words spoken by Our Lord about the universality of His Sacrifice from St. Luke, St. John and St. Paul and puts them together in the Consecration. But only people who kept untrammelled their Catholic Faith will accept that the Church can do that. If it is denied that Christ has ever said 'that His Blood was shed for all men', or if it is alleged that the Church in the 20th century has *not* got the power to take His words from different parts of Scripture and put them together as spoken by Him, then *Faith in the Church has been impaired*, and it is then utterly futile to rely heavily on the conviction that only Pope St. Pius V had that power.

The New Testament has actually stated that the Sacrifice of Christ's Passion and Death is for the redemption of the whole world, and so the Church did not put a lie in the words of the Consecration.

And what, I ask, is more beautiful than to contemplate the magnificent harmony that the Catholic Church of our times has effected? Both expressions, '*pro multis*', 'for the many', and '*for all men*', have given rise to difficulties. 'Pro multis', as we saw, became accepted by the 'Tridentiners' as meaning exclusively that the Sacrifice of the Mass was only offered for those who would in time avail themselves of its fruits: the grace for repentance and conversion. 'For all men' is explained away by the same people as *always* meaning 'that all men will be saved'. Undaunted, the Catholic Church now puts before us **both** renderings:

- In the *Missa Normativa*, the Latin Mass in the *Novus Ordo*, She reminds us by the use of the words '*pro multis*' that *not* all men are saved, but that *many* will avail themselves of the graces necessary to enter eternal salvation, the subjective Redemption.

- In the vernacular She teaches us that Christ's Blood, both in His Sacrifice on Calvary as in the Sacrifice of the Mass is offered to the Father so that sins *may* be forgiven. The objective Redemption.

'*Pro multis*' made the 'Tridentiners' complacent because it allowed some Jansenistic predestination to creep in into its use and explanation.

'*For all men*' makes our Modernists complacent, because of their thinking associated with their conviction that all will be saved and that no one will go to hell.

The true Catholic Spirit rejects both excesses and works hard to extend God's Salvation as far and as wide as possible.

(2) The second aspect in this controversy between the old and the new Mass format which pertains directly to Catholic Faith, is the appeal the Latin Massers make to a Pope, Pope St. Pius V. But an appeal to a Pope is an appeal to the Papacy itself, and the appeal to one Pope can never be played out against the authority of another Pope. If 'Tridentiners' appeal to Pope St. Pius V to 'prove' Pope Paul VI wrong, then they are placing Pope Paul outside the Papacy. That is what it has come to, and that is why Catholic Faith in Pope Paul VI is now directly involved.

Christ clearly gave to His successor on earth "the power to bind **and to undo**": "*All* that you shall undo on earth shall be considered undone in heaven". With that we have the Divine guarantee that no Pope will ever undo what cannot be undone in heaven. Unfortunately for the 'Tridentiners', but we thank God for His Providence that we know now with infallible certainty that Pope Pius V is a *Saint* in heaven. Meaning that Pope St. Pius V will now be the first to consider his own Bull *Quo Primum* undone. And what is more, true to the *Our Father*, he is now teaching us '*to do God's Will on earth as it is done in Heaven*'. For there, according to

Christ's own words, *Quo Primum* is now considered undone since it was undone by Pope Paul in a matter over which he, as Pope, had complete jurisdiction.

In fact, we can even go further and quite legitimately claim that *Quo Primum* was undone by the very Pope who gave it to the Church, Pope St. Pius V, since it was undone by the Papacy, which makes the name of the Holy Father immaterial from then on, since every Pope carries the name of the first Pope, Peter. And if any appeal is made to him, then Pope Pius V will remind all of us to accept the verdict of Pope Paul VI *as coming from himself.*

If this is unacceptable then again the result will be a loss of Catholic Faith on the part of the dissenters.

(3) A final word on the position of those troubled minds who believe that, even if Pope Paul was empowered to make changes in the liturgy, these changes, according to them, have gone too far, and so can no longer be legally or validly brought home to Pope Paul, but must be attributed to sinister influences around him. These people can believe all sorts of things, mainly:

(a) that the *Novus Ordo* could only be valid if given the right intention, but that in itself it is

(b) Protestant and will lead to Protestantism and *in se* it is therefore unacceptable, which means

(c) that the *Novus Ordo* is at least doubtful, and so it is safer to use the Tridentine Rite.

Some Priests of this frame of mind reconsecrate silently in Latin after having publicly used the vernacular words of the *Novus Ordo*. It is obvious that no argument from theology will change this frame of mind. They must realise that, if their position leads to what appears to them to be a contradiction on the human level, their original starting point was **not** made from inside the Catholic Faith where no such contradictions exist. This means that a review of their *Catholic* position is called for. Since we are dealing here with the validity of a Sacrament in which the Catholic Church cannot err, this review must lead to an Act of Faith in the Papacy, which really is the only condition necessary for the reception of the Supernatural Light by which it can be seen that the 'contradiction' they stumbled over is only apparent.

Conclusion

From a small beginning to this ...

Was there ever a 'small beginning'? Let us listen to some words spoken midway between 1970 and 1978. In 1974, *Michael Foley*, General President of the Latin Mass Society (LMS) of Australia had this to say in his concluding address at the AGM as reported in *Newsletter*, January 1975:

"As in 16th century England we have complete subversion of faith, of the Catholic Faith, the Sacramental system, the Apostolic Succession. We must pray for, and support, Archbishop Lefèbvre in Switzerland where we have valid ordination of Priests. Fr. Buckley is there now and has raised the point of Apostolic Succession ... When LMS was founded it was seemingly simple. The Bishops wanted to take the Latin, this organisation was formed to retain it. With the *Novus Ordo* five years ago, doctrine came under attack: we had to expand our aims. Then the other six Sacraments were subverted, one by one. We have to fight for all the Sacraments. It is a problem of unparalleled magnitude. The Reformation was similar, basically. Now the problem is of universal proportions. We now have a universal battle".

Yes, from a seemingly small beginning: the retention of the Latin in the Mass, to a full-scale war on the Holy Father and the Church. In 1974, Michael Foley could not foresee what would be written in 1976 and passed around Australia in 1978. But he did acknowledge that the seeds had been sown and he was aware of the forebodings.

These then are the true sentiments of the people who, through a nation-wide appeal to Catholics in Australia, have asked us to come over to their 'church', to their 'apostolic tradition', to their 'apostolic succession', to their 'faith'. Over the years their attitude and their loyalty and apologies for Archbishop Lefèbvre have hardened almost to the point of no return.

As this little book has tried to show, there are other answers to the problems they raise.

The Year 2000

It is now the year 2000. Since 1978 the Catholic World had to wait for another ten years before the appearance of the Apostolic Letter *Ecclesia Dei* of July 2, 1988, and the formation of the Pontifical Commission *Ecclesia Dei* under the Prefecture of Paul Augustin Card. Mayer, OSB.

In his 1991 letter to the American Bishops, the Cardinal Prefect puts the formation of the Commission in context. The following words taken from that letter are of great significance to understand the problem of the Holy Father and the Curia in the lead-up to Archbishop Lefèbvre's defection on June 30, 1988 and the issuing of Pope John Paul II's *motu proprio* three days later.

Card. Mayer wrote:

"On October 3, 1984, the Sacred Congregation for Divine Worship issued *Quattuor abhinc annos* in which the Holy Father granted the diocesan bishops *"the possibility of using an **indult** whereby priests and faithful...may be able to celebrate Mass by using the Roman Missal according to the 1962 edition"*.

The following conditions were stipulated:

- that those requesting permission do not *"call into question the legitimacy and doctrinal exactitude of the Roman Missal promulgated by Pope Paul VI in 1970"*, ..."As you well know, in response to the illicit ordination of bishops at Econe on June 30, 1988, and wishing to uphold the principles which had been established in the previous and unfortunately unfruitful dialogue with Archbishop Marcel

Lefèbvre, the Holy Father issued *Ecclesia Dei* on July 2, 1988.

• While insisting that the root of the schismatic act of Archbishop Lefèbvre lies in an *"incomplete and contradictory notion of Tradition"*, which fails to *"take sufficiently into account the living character of Tradition* (no. 4)

Consequently we wish to encourage to facilitate the proper and reverend celebration of the liturgical rites according to the Roman Missal of 1962 wherever there is a *genuine* desire for this on the part of the priests and faithful. This should not be construed as a promotion of that Missal in prejudice to the one promulgated eight years later, but simply a pastoral provision to meet the *rightful aspirations* of those who wish to worship according to the Latin liturgical tradition as celebrated for centuries ..."

In 1988 the Holy See had an open schism on its hands. The burning question was: 'what to do with those priests and lay people who for nearly 18 years had followed Archbishop Marcel Lefèbvre in his opposition to the Papal implementations of Vatican II mainly in the field of liturgy, ecumenism and freedom of religion, which, going by the above-quoted letter, the Holy See sees as legitimate and of doctrinal exactitude'?

It is obvious that the Holy Father John Paul II during the upheavals of his long pontificate has seen it as a major obligation laid upon his shoulders to avoid schisms of one kind or another by steering a conciliatory course of action. The Supreme Pontiff is acutely aware that in our strife-torn world nothing, absolutely nothing can be legitimately invoked as an excuse for the loss of one's eternal salvation. Only **sin** and **error** are forever excluded from this all-embracing view. No wrangling over Communion in the hand, no strife over altar girls, no war-to-death over 'evolution' (except where it is in error), no heartbreak over liturgy will ever be worthy to come between the Heavenly Father and His children.

And so the groping of the Holy See in 1984 to come to grips with the enormity of the threatening split in the Church over Archbishop Marcel Lefèbvre's war on the *Novus Ordo* revolved around this principle of unity where no *sin* or *error* are involved. Since it is no sin to love the old Latin Rite as long as it did not involve questioning and rejection of the new one, the solution was seen in granting an *indult* to those who were in serious danger of splitting away from Church unity.

In his Apostolic Letter *Ecclesia Dei* the Holy Father shows that he is well aware that the *thinking* of Archbishop Lefèbvre and his die-hard followers was in serious *error*, and so could *not* be taken into account in the granting of an *indult*. But since Oct. 3, 1984 it took another four years until, in 1988, the Archbishop brought things to a head with his schismatic act of ordaining bishops, and split his followers into two camps: those who agreed with his illegitimate action and those who did not. The way was now open to make a serious effort to regain at least the loyalty of the second group, in the hope that in time their thinking would gradually divest itself from error. The Holy Church never probes into the private forum of the soul where it is in relationship with God, except when in the confessional a matter is raised which obliges a Father Confessor to ascertain the honesty and sincerity of the penitent. The Holy Father knows that this laborious process of assimilation takes time and differs from person to person, which means that his life buoy of *Ecclesia Dei* may have been thrown to quite a number of insincere Catholics who privately still think that the Holy Spirit guided Vatican II in the wrong direction; that the Church was wrong in giving us the *Novus Ordo*, and that the New Mass is doubtful and must be avoided.

However, their troubles have no effect on the status of the principle which stands as a monument to Pope John Paul's governance of the Catholic Church in maybe the most difficult time in its glorious history:

- no doubting of the Holy Spirit's absolute protection against error in Vatican II;
- consequently, a genuine acceptance *in toto* of all the Decrees of Vatican II;
- the acceptance in Faith, shown in words and deeds, of the validity and legitimacy of the *Novus Ordo*;
- the full acceptance of the authority of Pope Paul VI.

Going by the glib and candid admissions made by the membership of the offshoot of the earlier Latin Mass Societies, the present-day movement *Una Voce*, the first one of these four seems to be the most difficult to accept.

Postscript

Letter of Dario Cardinal Castrillon Hoyos, President of the Papal Commission Ecclesia Dei, to the General Chapter of the Priestly Fraternity of St. Peter

"My very dear Brethren:

Your Fraternity is holding at the moment its General Chapter. In my position as the new President of the Papal Commission *Ecclesia Dei*, I would gladly be with you, in order to speak to you personally. Because this is not possible, due to obligations which I assumed quite some time ago, I am writing you this letter.

The General Chapter of your Fraternity is a privileged moment [in which] to look, together as brethren, upon the exalted Person of our Redeemer and only Lord, Jesus Christ. It is a privileged moment of Trinitarian communion, in which the unity of the Church of Our Lord and the unity among us as brethren strengthens itself. As disciples of Jesus, we must strive for perfection, but with the priorities which the Master has Himself revealed to us. The absolute priority is the love of God and the love of our brethren, as distinguishing characteristics of our Family of Faith. The love of God expresses itself in prayer, in the celebration of the Faith, in holding firm to certainties which concern the moral life, and in the disciplinary manifestations which protect and guarantee them. This is the special field of your particular place in the Church. Holding fast to the noble traditions in the celebration of the Divine Cult is its characteristic mark.

Since my appointment last April, I have studied the acts [or: archives] of your Institute. I have spoken with several of you, and I have read numerous letters which have reached me. Likewise, I have informed myself through people in Rome who have been familiar with your situation for years. After all of this, I would like to communicate to you my reflection and my decisions.

One cannot possibly deny that your Institute has been living through a severe crisis for a certain amount of time. A first attempt to solve this crisis was undertaken in February with the General Convocation held at Rocca di Papa. This [Convocation], as you know, worked out a compromise, which attempted to reconcile the demands of the General Law of the Church with the particular character of your Institute, and so to overcome your divisions. This compromise, unfortunately, has become the object of new controversies between those who accept it, and those who reject it.

In spite of this, the Superiors requested that the Papal Commission approve this compromise, and to make it a particular law for you. After mature reflection, and questioning of the experts, I ascertained that this is not possible.

The ground for this is the clear circumstances of the legal situation in this matter, namely:

A priest, who enjoys the privilege to celebrate the Mass according to the old Missal of 1962, does not lose the right, likewise to use the Missal of 1970, which is officially in force in the Latin Church. No Superior beneath the Supreme Pontiff can hinder a priest from following the General Law, which was promulgated by the Supreme Legislator, namely, to celebrate in the reformed Rite of Pope Paul VI.

It [i.e., the limitation or restriction] also cannot be imposed upon seminarians, <u>or be the reason for denying them ordination</u>. You know very well, that this last point is of great importance for you in this moment, when not a negligible number of seminarians and even priests have the intention to depart from your Institute, if this rule were imposed upon them---which, however, is in fact not possible.

It is therefore urgently necessary to render certain decisions, in order to avoid the falling apart of your Fraternity, and [to avoid] the loss of vocations, which are so precious in our time.

1.   The first decision is of juridical nature. Your Constitutions, <u>which were approved 'ad experimentum'</u> [ie., experimentally, temporarily], leave open the question of the possible number of terms of appointment for a Superior General. It appears appropriate to restrict these to two terms of six years each---that is, a maximum of twelve years---to bring the Fraternity into harmony with the majority of other religious Institutes. The competent authority of the Holy See hereby limits the term of office of the Superior General of the Priestly Fraternity of St. Peter to two successive terms of six years each. This Papal Commission thanks Father Bisig, who has exercised this function for twelve years, for everything which he has done for the Fraternity, which owes to him its consolidation and its expansion into several countries during the initial period of its history, as the fruit of his burning zeal and his desire for personal and collective sanctification. He will always be, through his experience, a pillar and support for your Fraternity and will, I am certain, help his successor through his good advice.

2.   The second decision is the following: It is known to you
that in 1991, Cardinal Innocenti, who was then President of this
Papal Commission, named Fr. Bisig to a further term of three years
as Superior General, despite a differing vote of the General Chapter. The conflict-ridden situation of your Fraternity presently demands a similar intervention of superior authority, in view of the
danger that an election could become the source of even more profound divisions. For this reason, I name Fr. Arnaud Devillers as
Superior General of the Priestly Fraternity of St. Peter for a term of
six years. Fr. Devillers fulfills the necessary conditions and knows
your Fraternity well from the inside. He has long experience as the
one responsible for the North American District, which he founded, and which he has firmly implanted in several American dioces-
es---always in good cooperation with the respective bishops. His
first assignment will be to re-establish peace in your Fraternity, by
working to maintain your common spirituality, and even to
strengthen it; likewise to reinforce your family spirit.

3.   The third decision concerns the Seminary at Wigratzbad.
Together with the one in the United States, it is the cradle of future
vocations. One must therefore give it the possibility to form priests
in all peace and calm, and to provide a solid theological and pastoral formation. For this reason, a new Rector will be named for the
International Seminary of St. Peter at Wigratzbad. He will dedicate
himself to the task of priestly formation, together with the college
of professors, whom he will select with the consent of the Superior
General. It is important that the seminarians find here a spiritual
atmosphere, a good spirit, professors adequate to their assignment,

and an exemplary ecclesial spirit, which carefully avoids all extremism. You know quite well that your Seminary is observed by many people in the Church, and that it must be exemplary in all respects. In particular, <u>it is required to avoid and combat a certain spirit of rebellion against the present-day Church</u>, which spirit easily finds followers among the young students, who---like all young people---already incline to extreme and rigorist positions. It is necessary, on the contrary, to cultivate love for the Church and Her Supreme Pastor, and to listen to Her Magisterium. <u>One cannot live in the Church and at the same time distance himself from Her</u>. (emphasis added)

The Superior General will likewise select a Rector for the American Seminary, for which the same findings are valid as for Wigratzbad.

I wish that all members of the Fraternity accept these decisions with submission and humility. May they all keep themselves from again forming pressure-groups or groups of resistance against the line of the Superior General.

I promise that the Papal Commission will be from now on more present in the Seminaries and other Houses of the Fraternity, and will watch more diligently over their good condition. It may also come about, that the Commission will intervene anew, if this is necessary.

What concerns the Liturgy remains as it should: Your Fraternity has the privilege to celebrate according to the liturgical books from 1962 <u>in its own chapels and churches</u>. The priests of the Institute normally celebrate according to this Rite, *but they have the right---it is unnecessary to repeat---to celebrate also according to the books presently in use, in particular cases which will not be frequent, but which nevertheless remain dependent upon the reasonable and tactful decision of the priests. I encourage you to concelebrate with the diocesan bishop, particularly on Maundy Thursday.*

In this way, you will visibly demonstrate your unity with the Pastor of the local Church---who is also your Pastor---and with his clergy, to whom those priests also belong who are members of Institutes of Consecrated Life or---as your Fraternity---of Communities of Apostolic Life, which have a pastoral charge in the diocese.

On the other hand, it is clear that no priest is obliged to make use of this right. In this way, an atmosphere of freedom and trust can arise in this area, which stands in opposition to every exclusivity and every liturgical extremism. The *Fraternity of St. Peter*, as its name already says, can only be a family of brethren, who mutually accept each other with fraternal love, and who are united wholly into the great family of the Roman Catholic Church, where there is a legitimate place for Catholics with a traditional sensibility, which I will defend with all my power.

I entrust to you one more personal reflection:

You must not view the aspect of the Rite [of the Liturgy] as the central point of the whole Church, or place this aspect on the same level as the fundamentals themselves,

such as unity in the true Faith, common discipline under the Apostolic Hierarchy, and the Liturgy, which is the celebration of the Mysteries of the Faith.

The Rite is not the celebration itself, but it is only one of the possible forms of the latter. Apart from that, do not forget that the Rite reformed by Pope Paul VI is the common Rite of the Church. It is not your task to alter this state of things, or so to speak about this Rite, as if it were of lesser value;

but rather to aid the Faithful who have an attachment to the old Rite better to find themselves once more in the Church. If it is true that the aspect of the Rite is an important help for the permanence of the Sacred, which in today's Church is so threatened by secularisation, this occurs not only through one single form of the Rite, as some might like to believe; but one must preserve the Holy in all relations with God. It is your task to do this, in that you celebrate according to your aptitudes. Nevertheless, you must not assign a priority to the form of the Liturgy, in which you have the privilege to celebrate. But rather, it is much more necessary to see this as the particular contribution of your Institute to the common work of the Church. Your contribution must fit itself into the harmony of the sanctity of the Church, where there is certainly a place for that which completes---not, however, for that which contradicts.

Insofar as you behave thus, you contribute at the same time to the New Evangelization, to which the Holy Father calls all of us.

I invoke upon all of you the protection of the Blessed Virgin Mary, the Queen of the Apostles, and the plenitude of heavenly graces, which God wishes to confer upon you: the Father, the Son, and the Holy Ghost."

Rome, the 29th June 2000
Dario Card. Castrillon Hoyos

The above Letter of his Eminence Cardinal Castrillon Hoyos, President of the Papal Commission *Ecclesia Dei* since April this year (2000) which is attached to this *Defence of the Novus Ordo Missae of His Holiness Pope VI* as a postscript, forms an integral part with the Disclaimer read out by the Secretary of the *Ecclesia Dei* Commission, Msgr. Perl.

Part of Msgr. Perls Statement to FIUV, November 1999.

[The following statement was delivered to the Delegates of the International Federation of *Una Voce International* at the organization's meeting in Rome, November 17, 1999.]

"Those who maintain that this is an abuse of power do not understand the true juridical situation: **that the Commission exercises the full authority of the Holy See over the aforementioned Fraternity**. To state that there is an intention to modify the traditional orientation of the Fraternity is not only absurd, but it gravely offends against the truth and the members of the Pontifical Commission.

4.   At the heart of this crisis is the problem of the concelebration of priests who are attached to certain forms of the Latin liturgical tradition at a Mass celebrated according to the rite presently in force. (*Novus Ordo Missae*). This possibility has been requested and occasionally carried out by some priests in Masses with the diocesan bishop, *but categorically refused by the majority.* The Congregation for Divine Worship and the Discipline of the Sacraments, after having consulted the Pontifical Council for the Interpretation of Legislative Texts and requested the advice of the Pontifical Commission *Ecclesia Dei,* has published "Official Responses" pertaining to this matter in *Notitiæ,* and has explained its reasons

to the superiors of the institutes concerned. These responses constitute a statement on the juridical level:

those who have the privilege of celebrating according to the liturgical books in use prior to the reform of Paul VI do not lose for that reason the right to celebrate according to the Missal of Paul VI - a right which belongs to every priest of the Roman rite. It is nowhere stated that these priests are obliged to do this, but that they have the right, and that no superior can forbid them from doing what the general law of the Church allows them to do. '*An exclusive right*' to celebrate according to the 1962 books *does not exist and has never existed,* and no official text makes such a mention. The texts of the Congregation for Divine Worship are very clear and leave no room for doubt on this point. *It is then utterly false to talk about taking away from the Fraternity its exclusive right, because such a right never existed.* On the other hand, it should be underscored that there is no intention of taking away the privileges conceded to the priests and to the institutes attached to the Latin liturgical tradition."

As can be learned from Card. Hoyos Letter of June 29, 2000, Rome is now fully aware that the sole stumbling block with the Priestly Fraternity of St. Peter is their insistence that an *exclusive right to say the Tridentine Rite does exist and that the members of the PFSP possess it.* No wonder the patience of Rome is wearing thin ...

Book III

Five Smooth Stones
(1 Sam. 17:40)

A Paper on Modern Trends
and How to Deal with Them

Frits Albers, Ph.B.

First Edition
April, 1977

Second Edition
July 1998

Third Edition
June 2024

Book III

Foreword to the First Edition

"I saw a strange church being built against every rule. No Angels were supervising the building operations. In that church nothing came from high above. Everything was done mechanically. Everything was being done according to human reason. I saw all sorts of people, things, doctrines and opinions in it. There was something proud, presumptuous AND COERCIVE about it all and they seemed to be very successful.

I did not see a single Angel nor a single Saint helping in the work. Then I saw that everything that pertained to Protestantism was to be spread everywhere and was gradually gaining the upper-hand. The Catholic religion fell into complete decadence. In those days Faith will fall very low and it will be preserved in some places only, in a few cottages and in a few families which God has protected from disasters and wars.

I saw that many pastors allowed themselves to be taken up with ideas that were dangerous to the Church. They were building a great, strange, extravagant church. Everyone was to be admitted in order to be united and to have equal rights: evangelicals, Catholics, sects of every description. Such was to be the new church, but God had other designs".

Anna Catharina Emmerich 1824.

(From *Life of Anna Catharina Emmerich*, by Rev. K. E. Schmoeger CSsR, with Ecclesiastical Approbation, 1867, 1868. On the command of Pope Pius IX, this book was translated into Italian.)

Introduction to the First Edition

In my efforts to expose to fellow Catholics the true meanings
and intentions contained in the writings of the late *Pierre Teilhard
de Chardin S.J.* (+ 1955), I have shown beyond any reasonable
doubt the wisdom of the Church in issuing Her Monita and Warnings against the works of this man. As time goes on it is becoming
increasingly more obvious, that his erroneous assumptions of Catholicism and of Science are being used for the false interpretations
of the teachings of the Second Vatican Council; that they are un-
derlying the notorious Dutch 'catechism' and the shady catecheti-
cal hand-outs based on it; and that they permeate the dubious seminary courses, weekend retreats, encounters and lectures designed
for the direct deception of countless numbers of Catholics and of
children. I am careful to note that Teilhard's absurdities are not
part of the fabric of all training programs mentioned here, but
most certainly of the great variety of the shady and dubious ones,
those strongly recommended by our Modernists.

If this deception is successful on a grand scale, and if Catholics
the world over are exchanging the priceless possession of their
Catholic Faith for this teilhardian perversion, then the looming
bulk of the "One-World 'church of darkness'", against which the
great Saint Pope *Pius X* wrote, and the characteristics of which he
clearly foretold, is in the process of becoming the ugly reality he
foresaw. No Catholic can remain lethargic and apathetic in the face
of it, because every Catholic should know, that the fatal results of
the loss of Catholic Faith are permanent. In the economy of God's
redemptive grace, the immense gift of Catholic Faith is only offered

and accepted once. This means that the ordinary means of grace: the 7 Sacraments of the Church, prayer, penance and good works, are sufficient to keep and nurture the Faith; but that extraordinary means of salvation, i.e. miracles of Grace, are necessary to restore this priceless possession to those who were unfortunate enough to give it up in exchange for some other persuasion. (Cfr. Hebr.10:26-31). And so for the ever alert Catholic, and especially the Catholic Priest, the whole struggle has largely become one of *prevention*. To come to the aid of those, who are in the process of going over to the wrong interpretation of Catholicism and of Vatican II.

There is a vast difference between "giving up one's Faith" and "giving up the practice of one's Faith". In the latter case the Faith is no longer operative through good works, but still dormant in the soul; in the former case, Catholics become apostates. It is well known that, in his 2nd letter to the Thessalonians, *St. Paul* refers to the time prior to Antichrist, '*the son of perdition*', as the era of the great apostasy, in which many Catholics would lose their Catholic Faith to a perversion of the Faith. Is what we see happening around us, the fulfillment of this prophecy? It seems highly significant that Pope *St. Pius X* warned us that already in his day he saw clearly at work in every country the great apostasy prior to the establishment of the One-World 'church of darkness'. Since in God's design there are no coincidences, we may take it, then, that Pope St. Pius X at least reminded us of the forecast made by St. Paul in order that we should do something about it. Since the words of the Apostle are readily available, I will only quote here once again the words of the saintly Pope:

"This organisation (i.e. the Sillon, composed of well-meaning social Catholics in France) which formerly afforded such promising expectations, has been harnessed in its course by the modern enemies of the Church, and is now no more than a miserable affluent, feeding **The Great Movement of Apostasy**, being organised in every country for the establishment of a One-World Church, which shall have neither dogmas nor hierarchy neither discipline of the mind nor curb for the passions, and which, under the pretext of freedom and human dignity, would bring back to the world - if such a church could ever be established - the reign of legalised cunning and brute force and of the oppression of the weak and of all those who toil and suffer". (*Our Apostolic Mandate*, 1910).

In any discussion on this creeping evil with its global ramifications, two things must stand out clearly and distinctly:

1. the supernatural, infused, divine light of Catholic Faith is absolutely necessary for the diagnosis and the prevention of this movement and its ultimate results, even for a full *natural* understanding of its causes, ramifications, consequences and ultimate defeat; and

2. in that same Light we must grasp once again the full reality of our free will: that God will not act unless through us, His Church and Our Lord's Mystical Body; and that our share and our glory in His victory will be proportional to our share in the struggle and the sacrifices.

For a great variety of reasons, many good Catholics have become overawed and even paralysed in the presence of the brashness and audacity of Modernism and Teilhardism, and have all but given in completely to the ruthless force with which their adherents assert to be universally accepted, and accepted as invincible. Altogether too many Catholic officials in positions of trust and power have cowered before the bearers of these evils in silent timidity, hoping that the night-mare will go away by itself, if they persist long enough in their ludicrous pretence that Modernism and its consequent loss of Catholic Faith is not there, or is no longer evil.

Understandably, this has caused havoc and confusion down the line amongst ordinary layfolk and Priests. Had not the same St. Pope Pius X stated in another encyclical (Pascendi), when referring to the Modernists, that *"audacity is their chief characteristic ?"*

And is it not true to say, that we see this audacity become more open and more brazen every day?

"One of their shock-troopers stepped out from the ranks of the Philistines; his name was Goliath, from Gath. He was six cubits and one span tall. On his head was a bronze helmet and he wore a breast-plate of scale armour; the breastplate weighed five thousand shekels of bronze. He had bronze greaves on his legs and a bronze javelin across his shoulder. The shaft of his spear was like a weaver's beam and the head of his spear weighed six hundred shekels of iron.

"He took his stand in front of the ranks of Israel and shouted: 'Why come out and range yourselves for battle? Am I not a Philistine and are you not the slaves of Saul? Choose a man and let him come down to me....' When Saul and all Israel heard these words of the Philistine, they were dismayed and terrified....

"David said to Saul: 'Let no one lose heart on his account. Your servant will go and fight this Philistine'. But Saul answered David: 'You cannot go and fight the Philistine; you are only a boy and he

has been a warrior from his youth'. David said to Saul: 'Your servant used to look after the sheep for his father, and whenever a lion
or a bear came out and took a sheep from the flock, I used to follow
him up and strike him down and rescue it from its mouth. If he
turned on me I seized him by the hair at his jaw and struck him
down and killed him. Your servant has killed both lion and bear,
and this uncircumcised Philistine shall be like one of them for he
has dared to insult the armies of the living God. Yahweh who res-
cued me from the claws of lion and bear', David said, 'will rescue
me from the power of this Philistine'. Then Saul said to David: 'Go,
and Yahweh be with you'.

"Saul made David put on his own armour, but not being used to
these things, David found he could not walk. 'I cannot walk with
these', he said to Saul, 'I am not used to them'. So they took them
off again.

"He took his staff in his hand, picked _five smooth stones_ from
the river bed, put them in his shepherd's bag, and with his sling in
his hand he went to meet the Philistine and the Philistine looked at
David and what he saw filled him with scorn. And the Philistine
cursed David by his gods. And David said to the Philistine: 'You
come against me with sword and spear and javelin, but I come
against you in the name of Yahweh Sabaoth, the God of the armies
of Israel that you have dared to insult. Today Yahweh will deliver
you into my hand and I shall kill you. I will cut off your head and
this very day I will give your dead body and the bodies of the Philistine army to the birds of the air and the wild beasts of the earth,
so that all the earth may know that there is a God in Israel and that
all His Assembly (Church) may know that it is not by sword or

spear that Yahweh gives the victory, for Yahweh is Lord of the battle and He will deliver you into our power'.

"No sooner had the Philistine started forward to confront David than David left the line of battle and ran to meet the Philistine. Putting his hand in his bag, he took out a stone and slung it and struck the Philistine on the forehead. The stone penetrated his forehead and he fell on his face to the ground. Then David ran and standing over the Philistine, seized the man's sword and drew it from the scabbard and with this he killed him, cutting off his head.

"The Philistines saw that their champion was dead and took to flight...." (1 Sam. 17: 4 - 52).

In this story David had only one enemy to overcome, and in the hands of a trained, young shepherd like David, each of his five stones was deadly, and each one of them, if selected, would have killed the braggart.

In Christ's own words the purpose of His coming was not to abolish the Old Covenant, but to complete it, bringing it to perfection. The story of David and Goliath will not be complete until it has served as a model and inspiration for the defeat of all God's enemies. God has many adversaries, and the five stones of David are a prefiguration of the Five Sacred Wounds of Our Blessed Saviour, with which He overcame *the* Enemy. In these Five Wounds the story of David came to perfection, *"and His whole Assembly knows that it is not by sword or spear that God gives victory"*. But in His Divine Wisdom and Goodness Christ left still very much to do for us, and so, although perfected, the story is not quite complete: we have to make up for what was still left undone in the Passion of Christ. (Cfr. Col. 1:24).

In this paper in the current series on Modernism and the defeat of the teilhardian 'Church of Darkness', I intend to put before the reader *Five Modern Trends* which, when tackled by any trained soldier for Christ and His Church, can lead to victory over one Goliath or another in the Enemy's strategy, and, when taken together, will contain more than enough to lead intrepid Catholics to the rout of the seemingly awesome and overwhelming One-World Church, and to the rescue of the victims from its grip. Or, as David put it, "*from the mouths of lions and bears*", to the greater Glory of God!

Foreword to the present Second Edition

"I saw ... that the whole world had marvelled and ran after the Beast. They prostrated themselves in front of the Beast saying: 'Who can compare with the Beast? How could anybody defeat him?'" (Rev. 13:3-4)

Shades of yet another Goliath, a modern braggart, to be brought down by *his* David: contemporary intrepid Catholics.

Introduction to the present Second Edition

The problem is not: how will *we* cope under Antichrist, but: how will Antichrist cope with *us*! For, ever since the first persecution, every me is a ME!

"Saul, Saul, why are you persecuting ME?" (Acts 9:4)

If ever anyone on earth had a problem, it is that 'beast' with the number of a man.

So, as was the case with the First Edition, we have once again gathered together everything that is needed to warrant a reprint of this little book.

Even more than twenty years ago we are aware that we have with us a monstrous 'church', that is, an enforced 'religious movement' which as a towering cumulous cloud, hangs motionless over the world of our times, variously referred to as *'The Church of Darkness'* or *'The One-World Church'*, or the *World Council of Churches*. A 'church' from which not many who enter it will ever come out alive to enter into eternal glory. For, at one stage on earth, to enter *this* 'church' one must wear **the mark of the beast**.

But what is the good of a 'church' without 'worship'? For that we go to the same chapter of his book of the Apocalypse where St. John spoke about the 'beast' and its mark. For in that chapter 13 St. John refers to a *second* beast, *"which has two horns like the Lamb, but speaks like the dragon. This second beast was servant to the first beast, and extended its authority everywhere, making the world and its people <u>worship</u> the first beast"*. Here there is talk about 'worship', but a 'worship' just as false as the 'church' is in which it will take place. For it is the 'worship' of a beast who is a man. Thus, next to Antichrist's political and economic movements, will there be a 'high priest' who is going to take care that the world's religious movements, other than the Catholic Church, will *appear* to look like Christ but proclaim the gospel of Satan, filling the *"One-World 'Church of Darkness'"* with people for the adoration of Antichrist himself.

And finally we will see on this scene the David's of God at work during this whole terrible period, intrepid Catholics, who, as the Church Militant, will, in their thousands, penetrate the colossal, worldwide humbug, rescue the captives and bring the whole façade crashing to the ground. The skilful use of their mental and spiritual armament is not aimed at people as St. Paul says:

"For we are not contending against flesh and blood, but against the principalities, against the powers, against the world rulers of this present darkness, against the spiritual hosts of wickedness in the heavenly places." (Eph. 6:12).

That is, against the whole might of Antichrist which has infiltrated the City of God with its errors and confusion, its blasphemies and filthy practices.

Since the first presentation of this paper, Easter 1977, the gap between commonsense and nonsense in modern living whereby nonsense was kept at bay is all but gone. The stark outline of good and evil for the protection of good no longer exists, while the dividing line between madness and sanity is just a blur.

Meanwhile our poor old world is sinking further and further in darkness. The prophecy of *Pope St. Pius X* made in 1910 has been fulfilled to the letter: a great movement of apostasy *has* occurred, which was characterised by no discipline of the mind and no curb on the passions, resulting in a 'religion' and a 'church' without hierarchy or dogma, and which *has* unleashed over the world a reign of legalised cunning and brute force, of the oppression of the weak and of all those who toil and suffer. Many striking details could be incorporated in this new update as examples of this chaotic state of affairs. But to become one more addition to the chorus of lament about the engulfing breakdown and misery was not the purpose of the original paper. The ingredients of this universal collapse of human life on the face of the earth are now visible everywhere. They are in no need of spelling out. Yet, even in the face of this universal collapse, our young men and women must continue to believe in Truth and beauty. They must not exchange their commonsense for nonsense as so many of their contemporaries have done and are still doing. They must not mistake evil for good, or embrace the modern madness as yet another form of 'sanity'. And above all: they must remain at their post without a grain of doubt, as placed there by God. The original paper was meant to give some of these insights to Catholic minds in need of reassurance in the adroit handling of the spiritual weapons of God against the powers of darkness.

Let us try to keep this second edition in the same orientation.

The sub-title of this paper speaks of '*modern trends*'. In the preparation for a take-over by Antichrist in the midst of which we find ourselves, it will not come as a surprise that many of these 'trends' have for their objective an assault on Catholic Faith. One of them is the impairment of Catholic Faith in the inerrancy of the written word of God, Sacred Scripture. This is dealt with in **Section**

I. Another trend is to weaken Catholic Faith in the inerrancy of Catholic Tradition, the way Catholic Faith has been passed on over the last 2000 years. This is being discussed in **Section II. Section III** deals with the modern assault from all quarters on "*the discipline of the mind*", that necessary substratum for a strong and sound Catholic Faith, whereas the subject of **Section IV** is the loss of Catholic Faith in the Dogma of the *Communion of Saints* with the direct result of the curtailing of Catholic resourcefulness. And **Section V** deals with one of the meanest mischiefs found in the Modernists' arsenal: their hatred for Catholic individuality.

The 'common denominator' of all these trends is *evolution*.

Section I

Moses and the Inerrancy of Scripture
as the Word of God

Although the madness of modern living is presently being propelled by its own momentum, it did have a beginning. One of the forces that contributed to the aimless, current spiral is *Evolution*. The attachment to Evolution dies hard. Its after effects are like the ones of Original Sin it denies: darkness of mind, weakness of will, inclination to pride and disobedience. It must rank amongst the most powerful temptations put to modern man, and its wholesale acceptance *as fact* is to be considered as the original sin of our times, through which the Devil got at the Faith of millions, and by which a *unification of evil* was obtained in preparation to one-world government and one-world religion. Enslavement of mind prior to the enslavement of bodies *and minds*. Some became convinced that Evolution is to be rejected on scientific evidence. Evolution is incompatible with the modern scientific advancements. As remarked elsewhere it has all the refinements of a crowbar if used on the ultra-fine balances of Nature discovered in the Atomic Age. It is also mathematically untenable. If adhered to by modern scientists, it can only be because of its inherent rejection of God and the Moral Order. Others became aware of the evil of Evolution when they studied the effects it produced after its introduction within the Catholic fold and its widespread acceptance by modern so-called 'theologians and catechists'. In those hands, the crowbar of Evolution became the instrument of abortion, the abortion of the Faith. The abortion of Vocations to the Priesthood and to the celibate and Religious Life. The acceptance of *The Pill* and abortion amongst Catholics, with its inherent rejection of Papal teaching, is directly related to the prior abandonment of the Catholic Faith caused by Teilhardian Evolution, even though the victims may never have read an actual book written by Teilhard. His spirit is soaked up everywhere, and unless there is present in the soul a great devotion to Our Lady, and through Her a great love for the Catholic Faith, the evil effects of the poison will become apparent, in some more marked than in others. And for many the only way that 'this devil can be cast out, is by prayer and fasting' (Mt.17:21), which reminds Catholics so vividly of the central message of *Fatima*, that once again we have been brought into the presence of the Mother of God.

Since it has been the fairytale of the so-called '*theistic evolution*' of the late *Pierre Teilhard de Chardin S.J.* which has been the vehicle by which our Catholic school children have been exposed to the thoughtless acceptance of *all* evolution, it is necessary, before we can deal in this paper with evolution as such, we spend a few moments considering the poison that has been injected over the last twenty-odd years into those innocent ears and hearts.

The children, especially in the senior high schools, have been assured that this one-in-a-hundred-year-phenomenon Teilhard has, with his teachings on evolution, single-handedly dragged the Catholic Church into the 20th century. "Look all around you", they have been told, "everyone believes in and follows evolution!" "It is madness of the Pope not to *be* part of that scene or not to *make* the whole Church part of it". (Remember? "The whole world is running after the beast". Sanity has become madness, and madness sanity!). "Even", they dare to continue, "Catholic Dogma is compatible with it!"

But that is not what Teilhard de Chardin said .... *This* is what he said:

"What increasingly dominates my interest is the effort to establish within myself and to diffuse around me <u>A NEW RELIGION</u> whose personal god is the soul of the world, as demanded by the cultural and religious stage we have reached". (*Letters to Leontine Zantha.* Collins, 1969 Jan 26, 1936, p. 114.)

"<u>A New Religion</u>??

"I have come to the conclusion that, in order to pay for a drastic valorisation and amortisation of the substance of things, a whole series of reshaping of certain representations or attitudes, which seem to us definitely fixed by Catholic Dogma, has become necessary if we sincerely wish to christify evolution. Seen thus, and because of an ineluctable necessity, one could say that a hitherto <u>UNKNOWN FORM OF RELIGION</u> is gradually germinating in the heart of modern man, in the furrow opened by the idea of evolution". (*Stuff of the Universe,* 1953, two years before his death in 1955.)

"<u>An Unknown Form of Religion</u>"??

These two quotes from Teilhard's published works go to the heart of the modern problem. Catholicism cannot, not even with the wildest stretch of the imagination, be truthfully called either a "<u>new</u>" or a "<u>hitherto unknown form</u> of religion". So Teilhard admits that it is no longer Catholicism in which he is interested or which he sees gradually germinating in the heart of modern man. Yet it is Catholic Dogma which is to be bent and twisted and re-shaped and reformulated in order to make *this new religion* <u>appear to be Catholic</u>. And that is precisely what they all do, the teilhardi-an teachers, the modernist lecturers and the "New Age" instructors in Catholic schools and seminaries, in weekend encounters and retreats, in seminars, books and periodicals. They twist, bend and stretch Catholic dogma until it means the opposite, and then the tangled mass is held up as if it is still Catholic. For they love to wear the two horns of the Lamb and be accepted as Catholic, but accord-ing to St. John and all good Catholics who listen to them, they speak the message of the devil.

No one but Teilhard himself could put it as clear as this! No one but Teilhard himself must be heard first on what *teilhardism* is all about! At least the man himself does not leave us in any doubt, in spite of the number of cloaks his innumerable followers may have found it necessary to put discreetly over the soulless corpse of his lifeless catholicity!

And that was by no means all he has said about this whole mat-ter. Here is some more:

"Is evolution a theory, a system or a hypothesis? It is much more: it is the general condition to which all theories, all hy-potheses, all systems must bow and which they must satisfy henceforward if they are to be thinkable and true. Evolution is a curve that all lines must follow".

(*The Phenomenon of Man.* Fontana (Collins), 1965, p. 241.)

Teilhard de Chardin literally means this! Even if God wants to be "thinkable and true", then He too must satisfy this curve as "*the*

soul of evolution" (as we saw in the first quote above). Here Teilhard places himself above God by allocating God His place in evolution, and by stipulating under what conditions even God can be
'thinkable and true'.....

**"Let us then acknowledge the situation honestly: Not only
'The Imitation of Christ', but also the Gospel itself needs to un-
dergo this correction, and the whole world will make them un-
dergo it!"** (*Le Sense Humaine,* 1929. In "Triumph Magazine". Vol.
VI, No. 10. Dec. 1971, p. 41).

"The whole world?".... The one thing that Our Blessed Lord and
Saviour came to redeem us from? The very thing that in time will
be running after the Beast? '*Correct*' the Gospel so it will be fit to
become part of Antichrist's "One-World 'Church of Darkness'"...?

"What makes and classifies a 'modern man'?" asks Teilhard,
playing on the pride of all who read him, and then he provides his
own answer:

**"Having become capable of seeing in terms, not of space and
time only, but also of *biological* space-time; and above all** (my
stress): **of having become incapable of seeing anything otherwise,
anything, not even himself".** (Teilhard's stress) (*The Phenomenon
of Man.* Fontana (Collins), 1965, pp. 241-242).

"Is the Kingdom of God a big family?" he asks. **"Yes in a sense
it is. But in another sense it is a prodigious BIOLOGICAL operation, that is, of the Redeeming Incarnation".** (Ibid. p. 321)

If it is fully understood what is being said here in these two
quotes, and what our children have been taught in our Catholic
schools, the mind boggles. The implications are truly colossal.

Using his favourite expression for evolution for extra emphasis, *biological space-time,* Teilhard asserts here that biological space-time (whatever it is) is the only supreme existing reality. It is all there is. *It* is evolution, and evolution is *it*! There is nothing else. No separate God, no Supernatural Realities. Throughout his life Teilhard expressed his dislike for the Supernatural, calling it *"that separate layer",* and blaming St. Augustine for inventing it. In the *one* layer God evolves with evolution as 'the soul of the world'. Everything must satisfy this evolving mass, this evolving universe, in order to be thinkable and true....

Then he makes the further assertion – and now we should really begin to wonder if we are not being taken for a ride by a madman if the whole matter wasn't so deadly serious! – that modern man, the modern Christian, the modern Catholic has grasped biological space-time correctly **only** if he, like Teilhard himself, has become incapable of seeing anything otherwise, anything, not even himself.... *No one* is to see himself as a child of God, or a child of Mary. There is no such 'thing' as Sanctifying Grace, nor, as we will see in a minute, sin.....

I repeat: outside biological space-time, evolution, there is *nothing* else. No separate God *"living in unapproachable Light"* (1 Tim. 6:16). Biological space-time is the home for the evolving god living in its *"divine milieu"*. Outside that god no other God can be postulated. The evolving god is part, the soul, of evolution. He too can only be thinkable and true if understood as part of evolution.

And now comes the crunch!

By inserting here the word 'biological', Teilhard has given us the origin of the *'cosmic-christ'*, that is, his idea of the Incarnation. The 'cosmic-christ' is – like all evolution - extended by biology, which in teilhardian language and in all modern understanding (married priests included) means: *sexual propagation.* Remember, there is no other Christ as we have become incapable of seeing anything else, including ourselves. *We are the 'cosmic-christ'.*

So at last here we have it all in full view. That which, according to Catholic Dogma, he should still be teaching but refuses to teach: namely that it is Original Sin which is passed on through sexual propagation, that he now transfers to the Incarnation and the Redemption, making both a biological function (and a prodigious one at that!) of the 'cosmic-christ' in his self-sufficient but equally and at the same time self-destructive system.

What a boon for modern catechesis: **"Redemption passed on through sex!"**

What all this does of course is lay the foundation for the rampant impurity of our days. This is how it is taught. This is the underpinning of encouraging masturbation, free love, premarital sex, the pill: *any sex* propagates 'the biological christ', the 'cosmic-christ'....

And we are reminded of the warning contained in the prophesy of Pope St. Pius X: *"No curb on the passions* in the 'Church of Darkness'".

Maybe there are still some teilhardian and modernist teachers and catechists left, honest enough to admit after reading the foregoing, that Teilhard's evolution is not what they thought it was. They may even go so far as to concede that the Holy See was wise to take precautions to prevent this teaching from penetrating the channels of catechetics and priestly formation, and they may even agree with us, that the spread of this corruption was entirely due to global disobedience, a true re-enactment of mankind's first or original sin.

But they may not go so far as to admit that evolution as such has been discredited by Teilhard's unscientific foray into it. In following science's lead which seems adamant that humans and apes come from a common ancestry, they may still insist in believing that lower forms of life can produce higher forms of life. They wish to feel in safe company with the great majority of scientists who dismiss the biblical claim that '*man*' required a special creation and that his *body* was formed from *dust* as a break from the rest of creation for which there exists no biological evidence.

Well, *do* we come from apes?

Did Sacred Scripture insert an irrevocable break to make Adam unique? To find out about these and related topics we go to **Moses**.

Moses was unique.

"Never has there, since that day, been a prophet in Israel as Moses, the man Yahweh knew face to face" (Deut.34:11).

Moses, as is related in that profoundly solemn passage quoted here, died with his vision and his vigour unimpaired. Would that only mean that he did not need glasses, or could still sire children? From the vantage point on *Mount Nebo*, Yahweh showed him the entire stretch of the Promised Land. But Yahweh had shown His servant infinitely more.... Here was His servant, unimpaired in his virility: still the born leader, towering over his impossible people. Why? Because he was, until he died *unimpaired in his vision*. Are we to believe, that in all those days and weeks, even months Moses spent face to face with His God, that God had never shown him anything? God knew the demanding role He required of His servant. To lead a whole people for 40 years through a desert; to sustain in them, during all those trying years, the Promise, not only of finding their own earthly promised land, but the Promise of their *Destiny*; to patiently suffer their rebellion, ignorance and quarrels: Moses must have been given by God a vision of their real value and significance, a vision which by necessity must have spanned the ages from one end to the other: from the beginning of Creation to their Conversion at the end of time.... And so God had shown His servant, His faithful servant, the Dawn of Creation, reenacted before him the Marvels of Old, and He asked him to record faithfully what he had seen. In God's omniscience Teilhard was there too, and anything that pseudo-science could throw up to discredit the Vision and its recorded image. And God made sure that Moses saw well, that he understood what he had seen, and accurately recorded what he had been shown.

And now, here came his servant, climbing unaided his last mountain, for his final meeting with his Creator, with his Vision unimpaired. After 40 years it needed no revision: it was not in any need for updating or correction. He had seen correctly: seen that before Adam and Eve there were no human beings on this planet. He saw the Fall, understood correctly God's Promise of the Redeemer, and grasped the significance of the Jewish phenomenon, then, as at the very end of time. *And the capture of his Unimpaired Vision within the Sacred Pages of Recorded History became the Inerrancy of Scripture.*

And when the Vision was on the verge of becoming the reality of the New Covenant, who but Moses was allowed to be seen talking with the Son of God on Mount Tabor and to see, as a reward of keeping his vision unimpaired, to see it incorporated in the inerrancy of the Young Church, who would from now on become the custodian of this Sacred Treasure until the end of time.

God loved His servant. He personally buried him there, and kept it as a sacred secret to Himself where He laid his remains to rest.

Now, all you teilhardians and kindred weeds go up to God on Mount Nebo, on this most solemn moment, and say

"*Sorry, God, but You gave the wrong vision to Moses. Teilhard tells us it could not possibly have happened the way Moses told us in Genesis. And Teilhard knows. He says evolution tells us a different story. And evolution is science, God. Science enough to disobey Your Church and to impair Moses' Vision....*"

"I see. And on the driftsand of what obscure backwater was this 'scientific edifice' erected?"

Like in the heady days of the Renaissance, our modern evolutionists must be confronted with the *Inerrancy of Scripture*. For decades now, the first eleven chapters of Genesis have been treated by Catholics with contempt. They have been reduced by them to myth and folklore, to symbolism and the work of 'primitive minds'. But God is not fooled by these feeble attempts to cover up a gross mental dishonesty. The big question remains: **are they prepared to admit that this reduction amounts to a *dismissal* of Genesis. Yes or no?** And for that very reason an insurmountable obstacle has been placed in the path of this dishonesty.

"Yahweh God fashioned Man of <u>dust</u> from the soil. Then He breathed into his nostrils a breath of life, and <u>thus</u> Man became a living being". (Gen. 2:7).

As can be expected from God's infinite perfection: this one-liner in Genesis is all that God needs to separate fact from fiction. It contains the circuit-breaker which, on the command of the Creator, was inserted by Moses into the narrative to stop any shortcut of evolution dead in its tracks.

No matter how many billions of years it may take the fancy of a particular scientist to dream up the moment that at last an ape chanced (and I mean 'chanced' here!) to become a man: <u>without the separating *"dust"*</u> between the two states of being, that particular 'ape', at the instant of the jump, would be in the possession of two incompatible *life-giving principles* or *'souls'*: his own animal soul of an ape (because he is supposed to be an ape, that is, *alive* at the moment of becoming human) and the suddenly acquired immaterial and immortal soul of a man. And that, according to the Creator of both ape and man is not only fanciful but altogether impossible. No living thing can have an animal soul ***and*** a human soul at the same time, i.e. exist as a living animal ***and*** as a live human being in the same body at the same time, or be in the possession of two entirely different and mutually exclusive DNAs. Thus God, in the inerrancy of Scripture, separated the live ape and the living Adam by *"dust"*, which means that, even in evolution, the ape must return to dust first, in other words must ***die,*** before Adam could be created *from his dust*. *"Remember man that you are dust"* (Ash-Wednesday).

We realise of course that for diehard evolutionists this impossibility of the immediate transition from ape to Man takes all the fun out of evolution. That's why it is good to remember that our present Holy Father Pope John Paul II has underscored the Genesis account by stating in a recent address to the Pontifical Academy of Science that:

"... the human body could have come from pre-existing matter."

All the tombs on earth and the whole fossil record constitute a huge but silent testimony of what is to be understood by *"pre-existing matter"*. It means dust. And with the above words the Holy Father states what Genesis says: **that a pre-existing life form will have to die first** (and return to dust) before it can be used as a receptacle for the reception of the human soul. And that is what Moses wrote down on the command of the Most High; for - as we saw - the alternative: two souls in the one body, has been blocked by the Divine circuit-breaker as altogether impossible.

This teaching of the Holy Father maintains his previous (1985) teaching on evolution, never more clearly pronounced than then:

"In its (that is, evolution's) **far-reaching claim, it is no longer merely a matter of the origin of the human person, but more extensively a matter of the *reduction of all intellectual phenomena including morality and religion to the basic model of 'evolution'* from which its function and limits are at the same time circumscribed. Such functionalization of Christian faith cannot fail to cause a confrontation with it and change it in its very core."** (The Pope's emphasis)

These words contain the appropriate rejection of what - as we saw - Teilhard de Chardin demanded when he wrote that *all* lines must follow the curve of evolution!

Just as the rejection by all the teilhardian modernists of only **one dogma:** the Dogma of Original Sin, resulted in the unhinging of **all** other Dogmas of the Catholic Faith ("<u>there is no part of Catholic Truth they leave untouched, none that they do not strive to corrupt</u>", St. Pius X in *Pascendi*), so will God deprive from Faith in *all* Holy Scripture those who reject His Word in such a vital matter as the revelation of His Special Creation of the human soul "*in the image and likeness of Himself*". God will not allow the Supernatural Light of Faith to be turned on and off at will by the proud moderns. The Supernatural Vision as contained in the Book of Genesis was given to *one* man, Moses, to sustain him in his superhuman task of maintaining in a sinful but chosen race its earthly promise as well as its Supernatural Promise, its Destiny, Significance and Vocation. That vision was faultless, and is to be respected and accepted by all who with Moses and Christ want to sustain the same earthly as well as Supernatural Destiny, Promise, Significance and Vocation of the Catholic Church. And to prevent, or overcome, any rebellion, deviation and return to slavery caused by Sin and Pride. How can any Catholic go after a poor evolutionist who is on the verge of giving up his Faith, if he himself is 'keeping his options open', allows himself to be immobilized between the two opposing points of view, which really means that he is already halfway up the road to evolution himself? He would fail to see that his fellow man is in mortal danger.

All of us are in need to go back to the simple Faith of the orthodox Catholic. Not only because of its simplicity, but because it *is* the most profound. God knows us intimately. He knows that if we hanker after the latest and the deepest and the most profound, where it is to be found. In the humility and obedience of the simple Faith, which so many of us overlook nowadays, because it looks such an unlikely prospect, so out of tune with the 'science' of the 'learned' and the worldly knowledge of the teilhardians. And yet, as this little essay has shown us so clearly, how often is all that merely superficial! Under the surface, deep in the heart of Genesis, lie the treasures of true Faith in the Word of God. How sure, and steady, and penetrating is the aim and accuracy of that *other-worldly* Trust in God?

It is our **first stone** that killed a modern Goliath, the unbelievable pressure that is all around us: to view Genesis from an evolutionary perspective.

Section II

The Mystique of Vatican II
And the Unbroken Tradition in the Catholic Church

We have seen that in his 1907 encyclical *Pascendi* Pope St. Pius X warned the whole Church about the Modernists that "*there is no part of Catholic Truth that they leave untouched, none that they do not strive to corrupt*". In Section I we studied their attack on Catholic Faith in the written Word of God. In this Section II we will have a look at their attitude to Catholic Tradition. For just as the natural understanding and the supernatural insights, which God had communicated as His Revelation to His servant Moses, became for Man the Inerrancy of <u>Scripture</u> when committed to the *written word*; so did these insights become the living <u>Tradition</u>, or the passing on of the *spoken word*, in the life of the Church which His Son founded. Through Divine Protection, this handing over of the Faith from generation to generation within the Catholic Church also became inerrant if presided over by the Pope of the day and the Bishops of the Church in communion with him.

Many Catholic and other bible translators are at present time engaged in changing words and meanings in their inferior products, because (as we have seen) teilhardian Catholics have a completely different message for our times than the Living Church has. This shows that with their different words and translations they want to bring us a different message, "*another 'gospel', which they think is the true Gospel of Our Saviour*". (Pope St. Pius X in *Our*

165

Apostolic Mandate in 1910). But just as it proved impossible to di-
vorce Holy Writ from its original God-given meaning and purpose,
so it proved equally impossible to tear this Supernatural Light and
understanding away from this living Tradition within the Catholic
Church. But *not* for lack of trying. The fact that Holy Scripture - in
the case of Moses - refers to these insights and this understanding
as a *'vision'*, makes us acknowledge the fact that Moses received
from God more than only supernatural enlightenment, and that
God showed His servant in visions while he was in His presence,
what was necessary for him to understand the Jewish phenomenon: then, as originally at the dawn of history, as at the consumma-
tion of the ages. Just so that Moses would be capable of sharing in
God's patience with his rebellious people as a true prefiguration of
Christ and His Divine compassion for sinful humanity, always ea-
ger to go astray. Since the Divine Redeemer was to be born from
the Jews, it became absolutely necessary that the Supernatural Significance of the Jewish phenomenon would be maintained and understood in the Supernatural Light of God's Revelation by all *"who
were in expectation of the consolation of Israel"*.

We know from *St. Paul's* description of Original Sin, from his
teachings about the uniqueness of Adam as a person, and from his
prophecies about the role of the Jews at the end of time, that he
took over the Mosaic account, ascribed the Original Sin to a unique
event through which death came into this world; and so confirmed
for all times that the same deviations which corrupted the Jewish
Tradition, would corrupt Catholic Tradition as well. If we accept,
on Paul's own testimony, that he spent some time in Arabia preparing for his mission, and that he received many revelations and

visions from the Lord, relating to the transition from the Jewish Tradition to the Catholic one, then it will not be hard to accept that Moses received from God the same profound illumination while he conversed with God in His presence. This then is the unbroken tradition of Moses and the Jewish people, which accepts God as the Author of Holy Scripture, which believes that the Bible is the Word of God and which maintains that the Living Tradition explains the meaning of this Revelation in time. It was this Tradition which went through its fulfilment, the Incarnate Word of God, into the Catholic Church, and which, through the Apostles, through the Fathers, through the Popes and the great Councils, through the Council of Trent and through *the Credo of the People of God* has come to us and will go beyond.

Now in those latter days, the *one thing* that, at the same time that it swept the world, also constituted the greatest *break* with the Insights and Understanding, contained in this Vision and its Divine Meaning, is Teilhardian evolution. The Mosaic account and the Catholic Tradition are definitely not evolutionary. It is no good claiming that Antiquity and Early Christianity knew nothing about it because evolution had not been 'invented' by then, for the simple reason that these Supernatural Insights and Revelations are *not* of human origin. God knew beforehand that evolution would eventually make its entry into world history, and so could have made it part of His Revelation. *He did not.* And evolution, even as it is, cannot be proven by ordinary scientific thinking. But in the whole of Tradition there is not a trace of it.

Yet what concerns us here for the moment is *teilhardian evolution* because it came from *within*. It is a human corruption of the

Living Tradition within the Catholic Church. Its fundamental heresy is a parallel Magisterium, equating conditional individual *Salvation* with the universal *Redemption* won by Christ, making salvation extend as far as Redemption. In his 'evolution' we are all on a cruise to god-omega, because it is **inevitable** that, through evolution, redemption itself becomes secured. Evolution is the 'home' of the cosmic-christ. Instead of original sin, it claims that salvation is propagated by procreation, thereby teaching that individual salvation and universal Redemption are the same, which flies directly in the face of Catholic Tradition which teaches that individual salvation is **not inevitable** but depends on human co-operation with Grace.

But for Western Catholics, grown soft on materialism, the fascination of this message of *'secured salvation'*, proved irresistible. Teilhard's foremost requirement is music to their ears and balm to their consciences. To be urged to embrace this world, in order to share in the incarnation of the cosmic-christ, as a pre-requisite to being swept by evolution *inevitably* into one's final destiny, who can resist that....?

This 'gospel' is of course nothing but the preaching of 'the great apostasy', foreshadowed by St. Paul, and pointed out by St. Pius X as being with us now. It is an absolute and final break with Catholic Tradition, which never taught the inevitability of individual Salvation. And through the inexorable pressure of the Holy Spirit, the teilhardian 'church' will in its turn be cut off and cast out from the Guardian of God's living Tradition, the Holy Catholic Church. The danger is that, through this great and universal apostasy, the separating *'church of darkness'* may be numerically larger than the

Catholic Church; resulting in the fact that this anti-church may take with it for a while the outward machinery of the Catholic Church in exactly the same way as, at the time of Christ's Passion and Death, the Son of God appeared to be the outcast from the corrupted Jewish tradition, and the separating Jewish Sanhedrin appeared to be in charge. And in retaining the *outward signs* of power and organisation, it was able to take most of the Jewish population of the day with it.

Having arrived at this seeming impasse, where can we find an arbiter with enough authority to settle this vexed question once and for all? The answer is not hard to find: we will have to consider here the profound significance of **Vatican II** within the living tradition of the Catholic Church. Even if this means facing up to the seemingly inexplicable paradox of our times: how, on the one hand, it appears possible that teilhardian evolutionists are so adept in dealing with the teachings of Vatican II in their own sinful, erroneous ways, and how, on the other hand, this great Council nevertheless defies and frustrates any designs the unholy ones have in dragging her down to their own heretical level. For an answer we will have to go back a long way.

Many an attentive reader of Sacred Scripture may have wondered at times why, in the Book of Genesis, there occur two accounts of Creation: one, in which the Majesty of the Creating God dominates, (Ch.1), the other, (Ch.2), more idyllic and poetic, in which the interest and attention centre around man, the first human beings in their earthly paradise, and the drama in which they became involved. This duality is not unique: it occurs each time a towering intellectual achievement is put before humanity. The classic Greek duality is the one between the philosophy of Plato and the philosophy of Aristotle. And so there exist within the Church two streams of philosophy: one, the Aristotelic-Thomistic system, in which the Church feels at home and which She has made Her own; the other the Platonic-Augustinian-Franciscan 'tradition', more mystical and idealistic, reflecting the nostalgia for the idyllic state of the Lost Paradise. In matters of such momentous importance it is obvious that such duality did not come about unless by the direct Will of God's creative Spirit. Why would that be so? God, the Creator of the human being, knows His own product intimately. He knows our strength and our weaknesses. He gave a definite priority to the intellect (just as a definite priority has been given to His most precious Gift to man: Faith; the root, foundation and beginning of all Justification), yet He knows that any 'towering intellectual achievement' tends to neglect the heart and human feelings, tends to lose some of that warmth, tends to become eroded, formalistic, legalistic, and in His Goodness He called into existence an in-built safety device, so that, when at some stage this erosion of heart and idealism would occur in the dominant system, the other more poetic and idyllic one, with its mystique and warmth and inner awareness could be called upon to restore to the predominantly intellectual system what it had lost in human understanding. But under no account was this restoring system to be divorced from the other one it is supposed to serve. It was there to correct, not to take over. The "human interest story" of Genesis pre-supposes the towering Majesty of the Creating God in Chapter 1 and not the other way around.

Now Vatican II was God's - and the Church's - answer to Catholics who had become too formalistic, legalistic and somewhat neglectful towards the needs of humanity in general, and of separated Christians in particular. It was an answer in the solid tradition of the Church to restore to Thomism what may have seeped away in previous decades, when the warnings of the Church fell on deaf ears.

Had Teilhard submitted his own evolutionary 'mystique' for scrutiny to the Church and to the bar of Thomism as an antidote for legalism and excessive formalism, he would, as a reward for his filial obedience, eventually have come to understand and appreciate why the Church was forced to relieve him of his evolutionary aspects as incompatible with Her Tradition, at the same time that he would have been very pleased to see the Church accept his concern for the human element as Her own. The result would have been that *the human centered interest of Vatican II* would have been anticipated by him, and would also have been properly understood for what it was by the next generation. The endless tragedy, however, was, that the inbuilt hatred for, and contradiction of Thomism, which characterises evolution outside the Church, was taken over by Teilhard as a necessary element - so he thought - to *correct* it, but eventually to *replace* it. But in discrediting and destroying Thomism from the inside, he also broke with Tradition. Vatican II drew attention to humanity's plight in Her own unique way, wholly from within the Church's Tradition, and teilhardism tried to do the same with an illegal substitute. That's why so many Catholics can be under the illusion that, in following the evolutionary teachings of Teilhard de Chardin's system, they are implementing the directives of Vatican II.

But that is not the whole story. All during the long and arduous centuries, the Catholic Church has kept alight the Beacon of God's Saving Truths, and has guided sinners to repentance and salvation in obedience to these Truths. Like Her Divine Founder, She too has had compassion with the multitudes and on the example and command of Her Groom, She has attended to their every need. But in Vatican II, it appears, the Catholic Church has shown this compassion for the multitudes in a unique way, but still wholly within the Tradition of the Church.

Only on two occasions in the whole history of the human race does it seem that God cast all reason and precaution aside, to let His Heart speak. The first occasion was, when He instituted the Blessed Eucharist, when, if the separation of His Body and Blood pronounced and effected there would have any meaning at all, necessitated His frightful passion and death, where this separation was made the reality it was in the Upper room. The institution of the Blessed Eucharist became the Signature under His own death warrant, freely given in a Love so surpassing all human understanding, that the great Apostle of Love could only exclaim: "*In fine dilexit eos*", "*He loved them till the very end*". Till He could go no further. And within 24 hours, the Sacred Body and Blood of Christ were completely separated on Calvary.... If this could not be surpassed, could it be imitated? Could the One who showed us so much love, inspire as much? Where would He find a receptacle suitable for such an inspiration? Where, but in a Bride, the Bride of the Lamb of God? And this became the second occasion, when, in an excess of love for that same sinful humanity: for pagans and Protestants, for Hindus and Mohammedans, for abortionists and homosexuals, for communists and freemasons, for teilhardians and modernists and all the derelicts over the place: for a whole world She had spoken to for 2000 years but never reached, the Catholic Church in Vatican II *"tradidit semetipsam"* *"gave Herself up as a victim"*; *"exinanivit semetipsam"*, *"emptied Herself"*, in the fine tradition of the Son of God. And within 10 years Her beauty was gone.... What took 2000 years to build was demolished within a decade. For, *on both occasions*, under the direct inspiration and instigation of the Evil One, there were traitors and predators waiting in the wings, ready to seize on this profound immolation as if it was a weakness: on the part of Christ, it was the Jewish Sanhedrin, which made the fatal mistake; and now in the case of the Catholic Church, it is the teilhardian 'church of darkness'. And just as in the days of Christ, a still uninformed but most loyal Peter took to the sword in defence of His Master, so in our days an equally fiery Archbishop Lefebvre has taken it upon himself to defend with the sword what he considered was the Church he knew before. Scandalised by Her disfigurations, he too made the same mistake as Peter in Gethsemane, and it is by now a fact of history that the Archbishop did not heed the command of the gentle Pope, and did not show *the same obedience* as the Prince of the Apostles gave to the command of his Master Christ.

The Mystery of the Catholic Church is so profound, that only the holiest of motives must be attributed to Her will and desire to follow Christ to Her own Good Friday and Calvary. The Catholic teilhardians, mistaking the Church's compassion for the millions as the seal on their own perversions, have betrayed the Church into the hands of Her enemies, greatly facilitating the global persecutions predicted by Our Lady of Fatima. In committing her children to these, the Church no doubt will have hastened the conversion of the world. And just as Christ in His Sacred Passion bore His sufferings in silence and only spoke to defend or expand His teaching, so the faithful should use the greater enlightenment which has come to them in their agony, when they see the Church they loved so much being treated the way She is now, to defend the Church's teaching, so that this Passion may not be lost on the perpetrators of the Evil. The Church is also divine, and so Her seemingly irrational act of Love to follow Christ in His annihilation for sinful humanity, must be ranked under the most profound acts of Wisdom and Sanity ever witnessed on this earth. The course of the Church is steadfast and sure. She knows what She is doing, even in acts where Her great heart seems to have gotten the better of Her great rationality.

In Section I of this paper we saw that God put a circuit-breaker in the Mosaic account of the creation of man in order to block any evolutionary interpretation or view of Genesis. Do we find the same circuit-breaker in Vatican II, placed there by the Holy Spirit to block any evolutionary interpretation of this great Council's deliberations and documents?

If we can be sure of one thing it is that Teilhard's evolutionary modernism got filtered out by the Council in no uncertain way. None of this was allowed through. It is absolutely impossible to maintain, even if force was used on the text, that the sacred documents refer - however remotely - to an evolutionary spirit. Everything is solid, traditional language. The examples one can choose are myriad, and can be found no matter where one opens the documents, even (and it is no exaggeration to say *especially*) in those where the Council breaks new ground. It would take us too far to give here even a few examples. So, in line with the above treatment of Vatican II's immolation of itself for the salvation of mankind and as a seal on this great Council's veracity and orthodoxy, I would like to remind the readers that in at least four places in its documents Vatican II urges Catholics to be prepared to shed their blood for the salvation of their fellow-men.

If that is not "solidly traditional" I do not know what is....

Maybe here is as good a place as any to say a few words about the new Liturgy. We recognize in the Life of Christ two sources for His humiliations. Some, like the Incarnation, sprung from His great Love for us and from His obedience to His Father's Will; others were inflicted upon Him by His enemies and came from the hatred of the Devil. When God revealed to the Angels in their period of Probation the Divine Decree that His Son, the Second Person of the Blessed Trinity, would take on human nature and become Man, many Angels were scandalised and protested. Until eventually the protest became open rebellion in the battle cry of Lucifer: "*Non serviam*", "*I will not serve...*". Cast into Hell forever, the hatred of the fallen angels froze into their eternal fixation, and it is not without significance that, in his meditations in the 30 day retreat, St. Ignatius continuously refers to Satan as "the enemy of human nature". For not believing in the human nature of Christ became his downfall. And so he became the second source of profound humiliations for Christ in His Sacred Passion, when for a while the Evil One was given power over that Sacred Body.

Now there can be no doubt that the Holy Father has made it crystal clear that the *Novus Ordo* comes from the bosom of the Church. For reasons deep down in the mystique of Her Vision, which, as we recognize, have a lot to do with Her compassion for the world, the Church in Vatican II, 'in emptying Herself' on the command and example of Her Spouse and Head, has not clung to the regal beauty of the Tridentine Mass, but has replaced it with the *Novus Ordo*. And so the *Novus Ordo* is one of those humiliations the Church has freely taken upon Herself. And just as Christ, through a freely accepted Incarnation, became *vulnerable* for all sorts of other humiliations which his enemies could now heap upon Him, so the *Novus Ordo* is also open to abuses which have nothing to do with the original intention. And just as through the Incarnation *"the secret thoughts of many hearts were laid bare"*, so also with regard to the *Novus Ordo*. The non-acceptance of it by the Latin Mass Societies until an indult was wrenched from the Holy Father to avoid further trouble had to be revealed as much as the disrespect and unbelief of the modernists.

In His Sacred Passion and Death, Christ looked for all the world like the loser. Yet He was never stronger. He became the corner stone, rejected by the builders. The corner stone of an entirely new creation, His very own Church. In rejecting Him, the Sanhedrin could make it appear as if finally *their interpretation* of the Jewish tradition had gained the upper hand, but all in vain. As we know: the Five Sacred Wounds of Our Redeemer became the instruments of defeat of the Enemy. In our days, the teilhardians and modernists are making the same mistake. They may *appear* to be in charge and make it credible that their evolutionary interpretation of Tradition is prevailing, but all in vain again. The *true meaning* of Vatican II, the immolation of the Holy Church as seen in the Supernatural Light of the authentic Catholic Tradition, will prove to be the **second stone** which will bring down the enemy and his cohorts at the same time that it will help save the world.

Section III

Fatima and the Discipline of the Mind

Evolution has failed. It has failed modern man. It has failed the modern scientist, the modernist Priest, the Teilhard de Chardin Nun, the liberal bishop, the biased college professor, the liberated women, the marxist social worker, the humanist catechist, the secular politician.

"Through means of psychological behaviourism, man is left with nothing that transcends his experiences. He has no values left and no morals, and his life becomes sheer practice without theory. But he consoles himself with the thought that life should be experimental. Modern man feels he should try all ideas since he will acknowledge no basis or yardstick by which to evaluate any idea, except trial and error which is strictly *groping in the dark*, which makes him essentially *an irrational animal let loose in nature*. In net: modern man is pathetically susceptible to making all the mistakes of these who went before him simply because he does not know enough history, enough tested principles, enough religion."

(John N. Moore, *Ed. D.*, in *Neo-Darwinism and Society* paraphrasing Prof. Richard Weaver's book *Ideas Have Consequences.*)

A man without a philosophy worthy of that name; without training in thinking: *a man without the discipline of the mind.* A man without the proper foundation on which a supernatural edifice of Faith can be built. An irrational animal no longer chiming in with Revelation. Or differently put by a man who should know:

179

"I am baffled by the way people still speak of the West as if it were at least a cultural unity against communism. But the West is divided, not only politically, but by an invisible cleavage. On one side are the voiceless masses with their own subdivisions and fractures. On the other side is the enlightened, articulate elite which to one degree or other has rejected the religious roots of the civilization - the roots without which it is no longer Western civilization, but a new order of beliefs, attitudes and mandates. In short, this is the order of which communism is one logical expression. Not originating in Russia, but in the cultural capitals of the West, reaching Russia by clandestine delivery via the old underground centres in Cracow, Vienna, Berne, Zurich and Geneva. <u>It is a Western body of beliefs that now threatens the West from Russia</u>. As a body of Western beliefs: secular, materialistic, and rationalistic, the intelligentsia of the West share it, and are therefore always committed to a secret, emotional complicity with communism, of which they dislike, not the communism, but only what, by chance of history, Russia has specially added to it: slave-labour camps, purges, MVD et alia. And that, not because the Western intellectuals find them unjustifiable, but because they are afraid of being caught in them. If they could have communism without the brutalities of overlording that the Russian experience bred, they have only marginal objections. Why should they object? What else is Socialism but Communism with the claws retracted?" (Note retracted, not removed).

(Whittaker Chambers. *Cold Friday*. 1964. pp. *225, 226*).

Yes, evolution has failed both modern man and modern woman. It has taken from the West any ideological weapon against the advancement of a new collectivism (totalitarianism) depriving the West of its wealth.

The whole chain reaction which *William of Occam* set in motion centuries ago with *Nominalism*, that the 'final product' of this whole chain reaction, modern man, would now love to see stopped. It was *Nominalism* which robbed Western Man of absolute values and absolute Truth, made him the measure of all things, and did not stop its run-down development through all the intervening ages because, as *Prof. Richard Weaver* so ably explained in his most famous book *Ideas have Consequences*. But stop it, he can't. For Western Man enjoying materialism as never before, without a thought for God or conscience, is so cynically atheistic that - as we just saw - he is indistinguishable from the old communist <u>mindset</u>, *and so he will live under it.*

"The Cuban missile crisis was the turning point in Soviet-American relations. It showed both sides that neither wanted a war and that their interests were not antithetical on all points. *Thus it signaled the suspension of the Cold War* and of the all-out insane armaments race between them. It showed that America had missile superiority sufficient to veto any major Soviet aggression, while the Soviet Union had sufficient missile power - in combination with the generally non-aggressive nature of America - to discourage the U.S. from using its missile superiority against the USSR. Thus was established a nuclear or power stalemate between the U.S. and Russia that secured each one against the other. This American-Soviet stalemate, by inhibiting the use of the power of each, permitted third powers to escape from the need to have power sufficient to back up their actions ... Part of this *return to reality* is embodied in the growing recognition that there are more situations in which the United States and the Soviet Union have parallel interests than otherwise ... The net result was the almost total disappearance of the world as seen by Dulles only a decade ago. Moreover, as we will see, *the aims, methods and structures of the superpowers were con-verging on increasingly parallel courses* (emphasis added)". (p.1091).

These words were written by the greatest living American research historian, *Dr. Carroll Quigley* in his mammoth book *Tragedy and Hope* (McMillan, 1966). They leave in clarity nothing to be desired. Complexity of the world's problems, the nuclear stalemate and the inability to control 'bushfires' all over the globe, made America finally face up to the reality that world **collectivism** is inevitable. A one-world government combined with a one-world 're-ligion'. This destroys the two pillars of faith the West deems necessary to enjoy its wealth and its unfair share of the world's resources without much thought of God and conscience:

1. the inability of a capitalist country like America to go communist or to finance the spread of communism, and

2. that the *Cold War* (i.e. the threat by America of immediate, massive nuclear retaliation in response to communist aggression) will be perpetuated.

As already remarked, modern European Man would love to see evolution stop dead in its tracks now, so that 'the claws would never be out for him'. And Quigley, the keen historian, has discovered, and told us about his discovery, that both these above-mentioned articles of faith are a *myth*. To Quigley, the Cold War is nothing but a smokescreen, behind which the Super-Powers have come to terms in power *sharing* because of the nuclear stalemate. The XIXth Section of his book is called *The New Era*, and deals with questions such as 'The Growth of Nuclear Stalemate', 'The Shifting Power balance', 'The Denouncement of the Cold War', 'The Disintegrating Super Blocks', which era runs from 1957 - 1964. In this Section, and also in the last one, "The Future in Perspective", Prof. Quigley draws the right conclusions from his accurate observations, and he clearly spells out the effects the nuclear stalemate has had on the formulation of American and Soviet foreign policy. He discusses the development of other forms of global unification: a unification in **fear**, in economic dependence through **starvation** (oil, money, resources, food), and in the political arena through the **erosion of authority**. All leading ultimately to a worldwide acceptance of some form of *collectivism*, which is, if it is anything, a nice word for *dictatorship*.

The real value of Quigley's book lies in the revelation, that America is powerless to prevent the spread of communism, and is now no longer averse to assist in the creation of a collectivist stage of the world. *Evolution*, on a world-wide basis, has brought modern man so close to atheism, that he is virtually indistinguishable from a communist. And so, according to Quigley's prognosis, he will live under some form of communism. The stalemate has produced the climate where collectivism is now building on this foundation laid by evolution and materialism, to spread itself right across the world in all sorts of political, educational, tertiary, parliamentary and communications institutions. And lately quite openly in the religious and ecumenical endeavours, even the ones started for noble purposes. So that we find ourselves heading, not for a colossal super clash between the super powers with atomic annihilation, but for a global take-over and enslavement, with America no longer objecting (Dulles), but actively helping (Kissinger). Since the unification through power *sharing* is infinitely preferable to nuclear annihilation, Russia and the United States are converging, according to Quigley, in *aims, methods* and *structures*. If this was even more apparent in 1977 than it was in 1964, when Quigley stopped researching and started to write his book, it has become far more apparent in everyday living in the nineties.

Yes, evolution has failed modern man dismally. It has robbed him of the *discipline of the mind,* so necessary to counteract the natural and supernatural evils that beset him all around. The salvation of the world literally depends on the few who kept it intact, together with the supernatural Faith, that can only be properly built on this sound natural substratum in order to enrich it even more.

So, if global collectivism is the reality facing us in the second half of the 20th Century and beyond, then it is not only good for our resourceful and intrepid Catholics to know where they are heading: to deprivations of rights and liberties under dictatorial politicians; to 'legalised cunning' and even brute force: it is imperative! Let us then, in the remainder of this Section III, analyse the two aspects of its solution.

Right at the beginning of the story of the persecutions under Antichrist in his *Book of Revelation*, St. John describes the apparition of a Woman in the heavens:

"Now a great sign appeared in heaven: a Woman adorned with the sun, standing on the moon and with twelve stars on her head for a crown." (Apoc. 13:1)

There is not a Catholic on earth who, on reading this, would not immediately think of Our Lady. And that was obviously the intention of the Holy Spirit, the Divine Inspirer of all Scripture. Even if the next sentence makes us reflect and accept that the great Woman thus adorned is also an image of Our Holy Mother the Church:

"She was pregnant and in labour, crying aloud in the pangs of childbirth. Then a second sign appeared in the sky: a huge, red dragon."

The Catholic Church at the beginning of the greatest persecutions of them all. And so it is the will of the Holy Spirit that in the time of Antichrist and in the preparations for this global subversion, the holy Catholic Church should be understood as being in the most intimate relationship with Our Lady, the Blessed Virgin Mary. And the Second Vatican Council has given a singular expression to this consoling truth; not only by refusing to have a separate Session on Our Lady, since according to the Fathers, She is an integral part of the Mystery of the Church, but also by declaring Our Blessed Lady *the Mother of the Church*, since they were guided by the same Inspiration which inspired Holy Scripture. And if St. John, under divine inspiration, could point out to us, at the beginning of the world empire of Antichrist, an apparition of a Woman in Heaven, so our Church, at the beginning of the world empire of Communism and Satanism, has pointed out to us also an apparition of a Woman in Heaven by approving the six apparitions of Our Lady at **Fatima**, Portugal, in 1917. The Catholic Church was not to enter the most terrible time of Her history without the special protection of Our Lady. And the elect around the world understood, and unceasingly, day and night, in concentration camps and hospitals, in trams, trains and buses, in schools and factories, and in households and churches, an uninterrupted stream of prayers and sacrifices goes up to the Mother of God for Our Holy Mother the Church here on earth. The global take-over under Evil is drawing to a close, but so is the global salvation under the Holy Mother of God.

But Satan understood too, and he became very pensive....

"And he placed himself at the shore of the sea...." (Apoc.12:18)

It is here that we have to draw attention to a world wide phenomenon: the spate (since the early sixties: the date is important as we will see) of whole series of unholy, unapproved 'apparitions' and messages, *Garabandal, San Damiano, Portavoz, Palmar de Troya, Bayside, Medjugorje,* which go for a while and then fizzle out, dry up, like the *"river the Dragon spewed up after the Woman, which was swallowed up by the earth"* (Apoc. 12 :15-16). Without ever coming to a <u>proper</u> end, they all go on and on without Church approval and with Church disapproval. And the greatest damage done through adherence to false and disapproved 'apparitions and messages' is the *scant regard* shown to lawful Church Authority. Self-delusion yet again at the root of another evil: stiff-necked self-will. For the followers of these unapproved apparitions will tolerate *nothing* to the contrary. By persisting in their delusion and self-will they hope to wrench from the Church the 'approval' they crave for.

The *one thing*, the *final* thing, all these unproved 'apparitions' talk about and warn about in unison is imminent catastrophes, in the form of atomic holocausts, unparalleled devastations and anni-hilations as punishments of Almighty God for sinful humanity. Whole cities are mentioned by name. Herein lies their hypnotic appeal to all their self-righteous followers: they are mesmerised by that. Because the world *is* sinful, and global devastations would ap-pear to be (almost demand to be) a natural outcome from this sor-ry state of affairs. *How, then, is it, that the Church can maintain that these messages do not come from God?* And what is even more incomprehensible: If all this is supposed to come from the devil, then what on earth is he up to? What is he after? What exactly is his game? What does he hope to achieve with it? Apart from the disobedience angle, where exactly are all these 'messages' wrong?

With those questions we have of course arrived at the most im-portant point of issue between us and Satan. Here we have reached rock bottom. These questions must be answered: there is no es-cape.

Why all these spurious, suspect, disobedient apparitions with their messages of global devastations? Why the smokescreen? What is he trying to hide? There *are* false pastors, and the messages *do* recommend prayer and penance ...

And so, in our grappling with the enormity of the problem, in our groping for the reality it holds, we are learning to formulate the all-important question correctly.

Smokescreen ....

If *Satan* is behind the building of this global empire, so visible that it did not escape the keen eye of America's foremost research historian Quigley, and if *Satan* is behind the building of this one-world 'church of darkness', so visible that it did not escape the watchful eye of a Pope and a Saint,

then what is the devil most afraid of?

In Who's care has the Church been placed since the beginning of this empire building? Who alone can show up his infernal plans? Who has the power to thwart him and to crush his head?

The answer is the same to all these questions: **Our Lady of Fatima**. Somehow Fatima holds the key, the clue, to the mystery of our time …

(i) It is easy to see, that all suspect apparitions and messages of our times have seduced Catholics to either *forget Fatima*, or to see it in the new light of the false 'apparitions', or to cover up its message under an endless stream of drivel, or to nullify it by their disregard for Church Authority. If Satan could give to Catholics *his* interpretation of Fatima, then the true meaning of Fatima would be lost. But this can only be done through false apparitions, the blind adherence to which is then a distinct advantage to him.

(ii) And then, with their attention riveted and glued by an unholy and almost fanatical hypnosis in the wrong direction: in the direction of the unapproved apparitions, in the direction of global annihilations, *away from Fatima*, he could then behind their backs, when they were not looking, prepare what he is really up to: *global enslavement* for which Fatima was meant to alert and prepare us, and from which it was intended to protect us.

But if we really live under the seal and sign of Fatima, with such an absolute certainty of the dominance it holds over our time, that we can throw back in Satan's face his *San Damiano* fraud, his

Portavoz fraud and all his other frauds: Teilhard, evolution, the false ecumenism in the 'Church of Darkness', in the full realization that Fatima and Medjugorje cannot be *both* and *together* true; that if one comes from God and obedience, the other comes from the devil, fraud and disobedience; that if one puts us in the right direction where, in the Light of our Supernatural, Catholic Faith, we can see the *natural* reality of our time take shape, the other puts us in the wrong direction, away from what is really happening, and away from proper light and understanding, *then where is the evidence for all this*? It better be good! We shall, in the forth-coming evidence first deal with the Devil's design, and then with God's design.

We have seen that, under the direct instigation of the Evil One, Teilhard de Chardin allocated to God His place in evolution. He allowed the Almighty Creator of heaven and earth to have the sub-servient role of being merely the *'soul of evolution'*. In speaking on behalf of God, and not allowing God to speak on His own behalf, he turned God for his readers and followers into a muzzled puppet of his evil designs.

Now if these minions of Satan do not shrink from allocating to God His place in their "One-World *'Church of Darkness'*", speak on His behalf and so canvass a muzzled God, what is to stop them from doing the same with Our Lady? In order to get millions of Catholics into this 'church' of theirs, they need a *'Madonna'*, but only an imitation one, one of their own making, one, whose 'mes-sages' are under their control. And that is the reason why this whole stream of unholy 'apparitions' must be compared with "*the river of Satan's vomit*" which the Dragon spewed after the Woman when She fled into the desert (Rev. 12:15).

The reason why Satan wants the Apparitions of Fatima "chased into the desert of oblivion" is clear.

In Fatima were confirmed all the Dogmas, the doctrines and devotions which have identified and set apart the Catholic Church for 2000 years for the spiritual survival of the world. In Fatima were held up and stressed the Dogma of the Blessed Trinity; the Divinity of Christ; the Real Presence; Mary Immaculate and assumed into Heaven; the love and devotion for the Sacred Heart of Jesus and the Immaculate Heart of Mary; the structured Church: Papacy, Bishops, Clergy and Laity; the Holy Family and the honour due to St. Joseph; the existence of Heaven, Hell, Purgatory, Grace, Sin, Angels, Devils; the necessity of Prayer and Purity, of Penance and Reparation, and of the Confession of Sins; frequent Communion and the devotion of the Five First Saturdays; the daily Rosary; the wearing of the Scapular; the reality of Miracles, the infinite Mercy of God and the forgiveness of sins; the Communion of Saints; Mary's insistence on the good performance of our daily duties; and yes, even Her request for Victimhood and standing in for sinners. And then Her final injunction to mankind: **"to stop offending God"**....

And with this we have come into the presence of God's designs when He sent His Holy Mother to the Portuguese hamlet of Fatima in 1917.

The absolute nobility of Fatima is brought out with crystal clarity from the fact that it possesses an aspect which is **unique** in the whole history of the world. Never at any other time in the whole history of the human race were three conditions fulfilled in such great detail surrounding a **miracle** from God, which was observed by more than 60,000 people:

(i) its **prediction.**

(ii) that it would happen at a previously predicted **date, time** and **place;**

(iii) to prove a previously given message as **coming from God.**

Not even in the prediction of His Son's own resurrection, the greatest prophecy of all times, did God include the precise detail that was contained in the prophecy of Fatima. Almighty God reserved this stupendous glory for His Mother and only for this *one* occasion. This can only mean that God wanted the Apparitions of His Mother at Fatima to be *unique,* and that God wanted us to know that, what Fatima is related to, and is pointing to, is of the utmost importance for all mankind.

[Refer to Appendix: "Miracle of the Sun: Astronomer's Verdict". Ed.]

With this it has become unavoidable to say a few words about one aspect of Fatima that has aroused so much heated interest: *its Third Secret,* if only because the devil's direct interference with it had for its immediate result the spate of false apparitions we talked about before. It is becoming rather obvious that, apart from the whole display of Catholic renewal contained in the Fatima message, it is this Secret for which the devil has a more than passing interest....

First, there were his satanic attempts to have <u>his version</u> of the secret leaked out to the world press in 1963. A 'version' of the secret was reportedly circulating in some 'diplomatic circles' in the West, finding eventually its way – of all places – to Moscow! It was alleged to have been given by Pope Paul VI to the Big Four leaders in the world: Kennedy, McMillan, de Gaulle and Krushchev when they met in Moscow in 1962 *to discuss the control of nuclear weapons*. And so, after the Third Secret had been firmly riveted with nuclear weapons and nuclear holocausts, it was 'leaked' to the press, and a German magazine printed Satan's version of the Secret on the 15th October, 1963.

Secondly, it became now of the utmost importance to Satan that his version of the Secret became 'substantiated' by *'heavenly apparitions and messages'*. And so the prolific spate of spurious apparitions, all of which sprang up after 1960, linked the published version of the Secret with the directions of the disobedient messages. That way Fatima became tied in with a lot of unholy and unapproved messages and 'apparitions', and so it became inevitable that, in the public mind, Fatima and its Secret became bracketed with imminent catastrophes, atomic holocausts, unparalleled global annihilations and devastations. That way Fatima had now been *'explained'*; it had become *updated*. Its Secret was now revealed; both Fatima and its Secret had been given a place in the smokescreen of the super-clash between the super-powers. Fatima had done its job it could now disappear, and the other 'heavenly apparitions' could take over *and demand full attention....*

But what if those bishops were right who, with their God-given authority, declared categorically that these other 'apparitions' did not exist? That they had *no supernatural foundation and origin*? That they did not come from God and from Our Lady? Then **obe-**

dience once again becomes of paramount importance in a most crucial issue. Because then it becomes obvious that Fatima has **not** been superseded. That it still stands alone; that it and its Secret must have a meaning totally different from the one Satan and the false apparitions are at pains to give it.

We can now be convinced that since 1960 any Catholic who kept his Supernatural, Catholic Faith, and the Light it gives, and who remained steadfastly devoted to Our Lady of Fatima, and who tried to implement Her demands, <u>and who refused to look in the direction of all the spurious apparitions </u>and in the direction of the Teilhardian church of darkness: that such a Catholic could see, in the Supernatural Light of this Faith, in the natural development and drift of life on earth (Quigley) and in the formation of the teilhardian church of darkness (St. Pius X) *the preparation for the reign of Antichrist.* Could *see,* how the basis for his political, economic, religious stranglehold is being laid.

One could not wish for a better description of what that same Pope St. Pius X has coined: ***"the discipline of the mind"*** here directly related to great fidelity to Our Lady of Fatima and to obedience to the **one** Church created in her image and likeness. For it is through this *"discipline"* that modern world trends not only are seen and understood, but, through the Light of Catholic Faith, are seen and understood <u>in their supernatural ramifications.</u> No wonder the devil hates Fatima.....

The Third Secret is *not* something that is given to a mocking, impure and undisciplined world to read from a piece of paper to satisfy its unholy curiosity. It is a secret that comes slowly to the attention of fully Marian Catholics who <u>see</u> with both their natural as well as their supernatural eyes what **Cardinal Wojtyla** outlined for us (Cracow, Poland, June 24, 1977):

"We find ourselves in the presence of the greatest confrontation in history, the greatest mankind had ever to confront. We are facing the final confrontation between the Church and the Anti-Church, between the Gospel and the Anti-Gospel."

And just as we can be sure that Fatima was meant to prevent all this, or, failing that, that it was meant to make us aware of it, to prepare us for it, and to mitigate it for those who had been faithful to its Central Lady and Her message, so can we be equally sure that the spurious apparitions did everything in their power to give these words a different meaning through their disobedience, even succeeding in making people spiritually blind for it.

For the reign of those who are behind this whole confrontation it is imperative that our earth is handed over to the coming world rulers largely intact. Obviously, the domination of our earth by the forces of Antichrist and his manipulators will not take place without local bloodshed and devastations. But Satan is not divided against himself. Through evolution *he* is the architect of both atheistic Western man and atheistic communist man. And if we are really witnessing the final stages in the preparation for a global takeover by 'the *Illuminati*' then it is not Satan's intention to make his minions the rulers of an atomic rubble heap. To rule the world effectively, which by Divine Prediction he will, he will need harbour installations, TV and radio networks, airports, armies, ships, power stations, factories, computers, satellites - in fact all the facilities 'modern man' (that pathetic end-product of a faked 'evolution') can hand over to him for his own enslavement....

And so, a great and lasting devotion to Our Lady of Fatima proves to be yet a **third stone** to bring down the enemies of God because of the *discipline of the mind* it gives to intrepid Catholics. That so necessary **natural understanding** of the things that go on around us as well as immense **supernatural insights** and tremendous Divine assistance to undertake and bring to fruition anything that is necessary for the victory of Her Immaculate Heart.

What is involved in this still needs careful examining.

"They are all of one mind in putting their strength and their powers at the disposal of the Beast, and they will go to war against the Lamb. But the Lamb is the Lord of lords and the King of kings and He will defeat them <u>and they will be defeated by His followers, the called, the chosen ones, the faithful.</u>" (St. John, Rev. 17:13-14).

The victory, by Divine Intervention, will be wrought by His human instruments, those trained and prepared by a great devotion to His Holy Mother. Prof. Quigley, in his book already mentioned, *Tragedy and Hope: A History of the World of Our Time* discusses rather forcibly what is involved here in the following manner.

After having pointed out the collapse of International Law and Order (e.g. the rise of Neo-Nazism in Europe) through the immobility of the Superpowers locked in nuclear deadlock, he outlines what will eventually take its place in these words:

".... efforts to establish automatic electronic decision-making on the basis of the growing volume and complexity of such information. This renunciation of the basic feature of being human: judgement and decision making, is very dangerous, and is a renunciation of the very faculty which gave man his success in the evolutionary struggle. If this whole process of human evolution is now to be abandoned in favour of some other, unconscious and mechanical, method of decision-making, in which the individual's flexibility and awareness are to be *subordinated to a rigid* **group process**, then man must yield to these forms of life, such as the social insects, which have already carried this method to a high degree of perfection.

This whole process has been made the central focus of a recent novel *Fail-safe...."*

And here Prof. Quigley gives a short account of the main feature of the book. After that he comments:

"The avoidance of the ultimate and total catastrophe in the book was achieved, *because a few men at and near the top, were able to resume the human functions of decision, self-sacrifice, love of their fellow-men and hope for the future;* but this should not conceal the fact that the whole world, in that story, came within minutes of handing its resources over to the insects." (pp.865 - 866).

This is profound, and one of the most penetrating analyses of the importance of Fatima for the preservation and training of the *discipline of the mind* one could read anywhere. For it means that, if the whole world is to be controlled by a tight group of very powerful men, that these men *will never leave their own decision-making* to machinery and computers, even if they force that sub-human existence on to the human ant heap under their control. It also means that, *to break this control,* equally clear-sighted human beings must resist this group control at the lower level, and with their gifts of observation, alertness, for decision-making, self-sacrifice, love for fellow-men and hope for the future, must come at or near the top of this power structure in order to wrench control from it. In order to do this, the followers of the Lamb must have come a long way in their love for and their training under Our Lady of Fatima.....

In conclusion of this Section with its message of overriding importance in the history of Salvation, let us see if a direct link between Fatima and the defeat of Antichrist can be established from documentation. Does Fatima really span our century, towering over Garabandal, Portavoz, San Damiano and all the other imitations? We can point to *two* prophecies by *St. Louis Grignon de Montfort* which are decisive to settle this matter once and for all. He said:

(i) in the defeat of Antichrist the ancient prophecy of the crushing of Satan's head by the Woman would be fulfilled, *and*

(ii) these times would not come to an end before Antichrist had made his appearance. It would only be after his defeat that a new era would be started. In other words: these times and their evil would culminate in Antichrist.

These two prophecies leave not much to be desired for clarification, and if Fatima is as unique as God wanted it to be, then it is here that one has to look for the answer. It is by these two prophecies that Catholics could have been in a position to discover the deviations from Fatima in all other so-called 'revelations'. Because they do not adhere to St. Grignion de Montfort's timetable. They are all full of atomic annihilations, etc., as punishments, and then nothing: just a period of peace. Then somehow Antichrist and the final judgement. But if this timetable of events does not come from God, since the 'apparitions' who peddle this lack any supernatural foundation, and since it is not supported by historic events (Quigley), nor by true prophetic evidence (Pope St. Pius X, St. Louis), then there remains only Fatima to be linked with the crushing of Satan's head, i.e. with the defeat of Antichrist. And that would then account for the unique importance of Fatima, and for its singular place in history. For, if only Fatima can be related to the culmination of our times and the defeat of Antichrist, then Fatima does not only span *this century,* but *all centuries,* right back to the First Prophecy in Paradise, where the *crushing of the head of the serpent* had been foretold by God. And this would at the same time account for the relentless pressure by which Satan wanted the adoption of *teilhardism* within the Catholic Church. For, if Catholics could be convinced that Adam and Eve are nothing but a myth, and the Fall as an event is unverifiable, then the First Prophecy in Paradise becomes completely hollowed out of meaning: whiteanted. But Fatima *is* true, and if it has the power in one blow not only to kill teilhardism, but also to span the centuries right back to the First Prophecy and Promise in Paradise, of which at the same time it is also its fulfilment, then it is no wonder that Satan will do everything to divert attention away from that. Because it can then only mean that this world is not so much heading for annihilation, but for some fate from which eventually only Our Lady and Her faithful servants will liberate us. Prof. Quigley accurately grasped the trend of world developments but failed to see their supernatural significance.

That is the *Tragedy* of our times. But our *Hope* lies in Our Lady's prophecy:

"In the end My Immaculate Heart will triumph."

Section IV

The Communion of Saints and Catholic Resourcefulness

After a rather long and involved previous section which centred on the necessity for the acquisition **and** the possession of *the discipline of the mind*, the following is to be clearly understood.

The term was coined by *Pope St. Pius X* in his often mentioned letter to the French Bishops in 1910: *Our Apostolic Mandate.* He made the absence of this "discipline" one of the hallmarks of the One-World Church which he both saw and described in detail.

The discipline of the mind consists of *two* parts.

The first of these consists of the acquisition and the possession of <u>natural understanding</u>, so necessary for finding our way here on earth under all given circumstances. The central core of this understanding is the commonsense and the realism of the philosophy of St. Thomas Aquinas, the *"Everlasting Philosophy"*. Since 'modern man' has turned his back on this philosophy, *John N. Moore* could write what he wrote above, quoting with approval *Prof. Richard Weaver's* book carrying the appropriate title: *Ideas have Consequences.*

The other part consists of <u>supernatural insights</u>, acquired by the Light of Faith, but only securely built on the former: the acquired wisdom of true natural understanding. The combination of these two components is so invincible, that only to those who possess them in abundance can the safety of the world be entrusted. That this fullness is only acquired through a great fidelity to the designs God had in mind when He sent His Holy Mother to Fatima is the cornerstone of the previous (third) section in this paper on Catholic resourcefulness. These insights and the greatly increased understanding they produce are *not* acquired by following and promoting evolution, or the spate of false 'apparitions', since, on the testimony of the proper Church authorities in these matters, they do not come from God. But the insights and understanding that fidelity to *God's* designs will bring with it, will in time topple yet another Goliath: Antichrist.

Thus the previous chapter was written to bring home to us, that a sincere devotion to the Mother of God will have – amongst other benefits – two great effects on Catholics and other Christians: it will greatly increase the Light and Supernatural Insights of their Faith, even to the extent of gaining a deeper natural understanding of the processes and tendencies of the times in which they live, as well as greatly increasing what St. Pius X has called "the discipline of the mind". Meaning, that living in close union with Mary, 'the Seat of Wisdom', will sharpen the human faculties of sound judgement and decision making, which will be a tremendous help to the Church in overcoming Her enemies and their infernal strategies. For the battle is being fought on some very down-to-earth issues.

Now it is obvious that the checklist above of what the Apparitions of Fatima were all about in the Mind of God, is worked out by any Catholic in the privacy of his or her individual soul. It is there that great Light is obtained in prayer, sacrifices and meditations. To see how this growing understanding and these insights can be translated into *action* in their own lives circumstances, it may be helpful to remind all of us how the Saints before us managed the difficult task of combining outward action with the so necessary inner composition and contemplation. They sure can show us how to have our priorities right. This translation of our prayerlife into action will be attempted in this present installment, Section IV. And on this the Second Vatican Council has something very practical to offer.

Because of an almost unanimous decision taken by the Fathers of the Second Vatican Council **not** to issue a separate Decree on Our Lady, but to treat Her as an integral part of the Mystery of the Church at this time of great trial and tribulation, the children of Mary will clearly see the Great Lady *in* the Church, and the Church *in* Our Lady. Due to this helpful guidance our devotion for the Mother of God (Section III) will become inseparable from our love for the Church (Section IV). This gives us the desirable foundation for the subdivision mentioned above.

- For the acquisition of the so necessary insights and understanding of what our times are all about, we turn for meditation and contemplation *to Our Lady of Fatima* (Section III.

- But then, for the translation into action of this rich understanding, we look at what the *Church* of our times is so desperately in need of. For, instead of losing contact with Our Lady of Fatima, we see that same Lady *in* the Church (Section IV), exactly as the Second Vatican Council wants us to do.

It Is truly amazing to see so many Catholics, who have survived "cyclone Teilhard", who successfully withstood the onslaughts of Modernism, who have no time for false apparitions, but kept untrammeled their childlike Catholic Faith, are found to have a singular devotion to Our Lady, and more specifically are greatly devoted to Our Lady of Fatima. The devout wearing of Her Sacred Scapular has re-enacted for them the wondrous protection by the Angel of God, who descended with the three young men in the burning, fiery furnace of king Nebuchednezzar, making the inside of this raging furnace bearable to live in. (Dan. 3:4-50). With this reference we have arrived at the subject-matter of this Section IV: <u>What is the Church of our times mostly in need of</u>, and how do the Saints help us in this?

In a time in which so many 'churches' and groupings are vying with each other for our immediate attention, our first concern, our first priority is to concentrate on the One True Church, the *Kingdom of God,* Our Holy Mother the Catholic Church, the Mystical Body of Christ, which, as we know, is *in* this world but not *of* this world. The grave injunction of Our Lady at Fatima: to be concerned for sinners and for the avoidance of sin, as well as for the reparation of sin, Is a twentieth century reminder of Her Son's command to us:

"Set your hearts on His Kingdom first, and on its righteousness, and all these other things will be given to you as well." (Mat.6:33)

The fact that Our Lady's solemn warning has largely fallen on deaf ears is the surest sign that by and large Catholics too have ceased to be concerned for the Kingdom of God first. And when Teilhard came along with his song: *"Build the earth, for that is from now on the Kingdom of God; that is now 'the divine milieu', and then evolution will take care of the rest",* countless Catholics believed him and went over to his substitute faith. In order to strengthen our resolve not to fall for it, we may have a brief look at what was the cause of that erosion.

Long before Teilhard's fancies were openly preached within the confines of the 'City of God', affluent Western Catholics had become ashamed of being identified with simple people whose first concern was the spiritual Kingdom of God. Thus it came about that this concern was left to Saints or to cranks or 'religious fanatics'. Self-respecting Catholics became self-conscious about their religious practices and fervour; and the childlike faith together with Our Lord's solemn warning: *"Truly I say to you: unless you change and become like little children, you will never enter the Kingdom of Heaven"* got lost (Mat. 18 3). This abandonment of the concern for the Kingdom of God, and the grateful acceptance of the fortuitous teilhardian substitute of 'Building the earth', has been hailed everywhere as a sign of Catholic maturity, of which the reception of Communion in the hand has become both the symbol and the excess. What was it that started Catholics off on this rather unusual road? A very unusual situation.

During the last world war, it was the experience of many Catholics that it is quite possible to collaborate with all sorts of people for the defeat of a common enemy. Religious differences became subordinate to the common goal. Even the fact that hatred was an asset and that fraud and stealing from the enemy were considered virtues did not deter them in transferring – after the war – this euphoria to other fields of human endeavour. The temptation to perpetuate this collaboration in *'building the earth'* appeared to be too strong; and it was mainly through the Dutch Hierarchy's approval of the infamous so-called *'Dutch Catechism'* that this false ecumenism and these erroneous interpretations of Catholicism and of Vatican II became respectable. Even if Catholics band together legitimately with others to eliminate hunger, poverty and injustices, their *main* concern remains the Kingdom of God, whose chief enemies here on earth are *not* hunger, poverty and injustices, but *sin, error, falsehoods, unbelief and corruption of doctrine,* the things that Our Lady of Fatima stressed. We have God's guarantee that making His Kingdom our **main** concern by fighting *sin, error, falsehoods, unbelief* and *corruption of doctrine,* is at the same time taking good care of all the other things, i.e. is taking care of *hunger, poverty and injustices.* "All these other things will be given to you as well". To teilhardians this is totally unacceptable; this concern for the world cannot be left to God and so it must rank in importance with the Kingdom of God.

We set out in Section IV of this paper to see Our Lady in the Church and the One True Church in Our Lady. We have now gathered enough information to see why it is that orthodox Catholics no longer see Her in the various 'churches' that are being presented to them on the modern world scene. In other words, we have now enough information to understand that none of the 'churches' mentioned below are a true substitute of the Kingdom of God, our Holy Catholic Church.

- Mary is **not** found in the "One-World Church" depicted by Pope St. Pius X, a truly Modernist monstrosity with no discipline of the mind, no curb on the passions, no hierarchy, no dogma, intent to bring back to the world the reign of legalised cunning, and brute force, and the oppression of the weak and of all those who toil and suffer.

- She is *not* found in the 'religious movement' of the second Beast doing everything in its power to subjugate the whole world to the tyranny of the first Beast. A true parallel description from Sacred Scripture of what Pope St. Pius X saw and outlined for us in more detail as being the 'church' of Modernism.

- She is *not* found in a 'church' where God has been allocated His place by Teilhard de Chardin: that of being the 'soul of evolution', in which 'church' evolution will from then on take care of everything else.

- She is *not* found in "Building the earth" as a 'church' of this world in which Her Son will never find His 'divine milieu'.

- Finally, She is *not* found in any of the 'churches' which did spring up out of disobedience against legitimate Church authority: those promoting the spate of false 'apparitions' and their endless 'messages', which were condemned by the bishops of the various dioceses in which they occurred as having no supernatural origin.

We may gauge from the throngs of Catholics who have flocked worldwide to one or another of these above-mentioned agglomerates, how serious the loss of their cohesion has become away from the Mother Church, the only one where Mary can be seen *in* the Church and the Church *in* the Mother of God.

In times like these great strength and consolation are given to Catholics who, under the impulses of grace, turn to the Lives of the Saints to see how they served their God and their Church and how to be inspired by the ways in which they overcame their difficulties and turned apparent defeat into victories for the Lamb of God.

The Communion of Saints, that spiritual intercourse between the Blessed in Heaven, the faithful on earth and the Holy Souls in purgatory, is a Dogma of the Catholic Church and an article of Faith in the Creed. The roots of this Sacred Tradition go back to the Old Testament. Vatican II, sensing strongly the corrupting influence of an earth-centered substitute for the Catholic Faith, has stressed with unusual emphasis the overriding importance of this Dogma in her Dogmatic Constitution on the Church, *Lumen Gentium*, Ch, 7. There is rich material here, and the reader is referred to this section for enlightenment in the traditional teachings of the Church on this topic.

Out of the legacy the Saints have left us from their lives in their work for the Church in fighting *sin* and all the evils of their days that flowed from *ignorance, error* and the *corruption of doctrine*, we have only room here to go into some detail to compare how *"the corporal works of mercy"* were viewed by them and how they are viewed today.

It sounds almost impossible, but it is true: marxist Catholics have hopelessly wrong ideas of the *Corporal Works of Mercy*, imposed on all of us by Christ. Such Catholics think that *poverty, hunger, injustices and inequalities as such* are the supreme evils of our times, and that the Church must adopt a more revolutionary, Marxist and teilhardian 'inspiration' in order to see and appreciate this new interpretation of the Gospel. With Marxists in charge of the WCC, they agree that *armed revolutions, force, coercion, deceit and violence* (unpleasant as they may be) must be accepted as God-inspired means, necessary to implement this new interpretation of the Gospel because of the intransigence of capitalism.

The great answer to this perversion is of course *Catholic Tradition* as it was seen and lived and interpreted by the great men and women who went before us. Never in the whole history of the Catholic Church has it been found necessary to invoke a perversion of the Truth, as is done today by these Marxist Catholics, in order to see at last the corporal works of mercy in their true light. The Catholic Church has always maintained that the unselfish love for God in the Kingdom of God is the supernatural source of the true love for our neighbour, and is at the same time the inspiration for the incredible richness in the manifold expressions of that love found in the lives of the Saints. From the days of Christ, the corporal works of mercy have been understood and recommended by the Church as a powerful means for the sanctification of Christians, as is still amply documented in the Handbook of the *St. Vincent de Paul Society*. Its members consider it a *privilege* to administer to the poor. For it is through personal sanctity, avoidance of sin and atonement for sin, that the Kingdom of God is spread and that evil in all its forms is eliminated. Spiritual evils first: sin, darkness of mind, unbelief, ignorance and corruption, as well as all the other misfortunes with which Marxist Catholics are so exclusively preoccupied. And so the Lives of the Saints, and of all great and holy men and women who went before, will turn out to be yet another stone, by which a brash and boisterous Philistine can be brought down to earth and cut down to size.

As previously remarked, sensing a most strong departure from Catholic Tradition in this whole matter of interpretation of how Catholics should go about the business of *living the Faith*, not only in the corporal works of mercy but in any action taken on behalf of the Catholic Church, the Vatican Council unequivocally bases Her teaching squarely on Tradition with the following words:

"This most sacred Synod accepts with great devotion the venerable Faith of our ancestors regarding this vital fellowship with our brethren who are in heavenly glory or who are still being purified after death. It proposes again the Decrees of the second Council of Nicea (A.D. 787), of the Council of Florence (1439) and of the Council of Trent (1549-63). And at the same time, as part of its own pastoral solicitude, this Synod urges all concerned to work hard to prevent or correct any abuses excesses or defects which may have crept in here and there, and to restore all things to a more ample praise of Christ and of God." (*Lumen Gentium* #51)

It is obvious from this that the Holy Spirit, far from recommending a modernist interpretation of how the Faith should be lived as is portrayed by our teilhardians, reminds us with the Authority of the Catholic Church Herself, to listen to the whole of Tradition of the Church in this vital matter, since Communism, Marxism, Teilhardism and Modernism are all and singly modern corruptions of the Gospel message and of Tradition, and have all been condemned by the Church. They remain excluded from the Communion of Saints as a genuine interpretation of how present-day Catholics should go about the business of 'living the Faith'.

Rooted in Tradition, Catholic resourcefulness then becomes truly unlimited; and once Our Holy Mother the Church has delineated the ambit and scope of this resourcefulness, She encourages every Catholic to work out, under the guidance of the Holy Spirit and of Tradition, the special work that is to be undertaken in his or her own circumstances; to develop his or her own style, and to be inspired by the efforts which proved to be successful in the past in similar circumstances. Since it is clearly insurmountable to try to go into any detail at all here, however briefly, with the intention of presenting some kind of complete picture, I will limit myself, at the end of this chapter, to an example already touched upon elsewhere.

At the beginning of this Section IV a brief outline was given why Catholics, next to the priceless possession of their Catholic Faith, should keep and develop the invaluable foundation for this Faith: *the Discipline of the Mind.* For it will be this human quality which will scrutinize everything and which will successfully guide Catholics to the top of any power group or organization which will succeed in mastering the impossible: *to gain control of our earth.* In those circumstances and conditions, Catholic resourcefulness will be severely tested, and will require years of preparation. Since this seems to be a unique case, where can we learn and study up about it?

God, in His Providence, has provided us with an answer in the *Books of the Maccabees I and II.* Although many Catholics and other Christians will be martyred under the great upheavals to come when they finally engulf our earth before the appearance of a great conqueror, it is nevertheless an article of Faith that *"the gates of Hell will not prevail against the Church"* and that an unbroken

Catholic Tradition will continue during and after the reign of St. Paul's *"son of perdition"* (2 Thess. 2:10). Since all of Holy Scripture is useful for instruction or refutation (Letter to Timothy), the following is presented for those who will benefit from a reminder of how things were resolved in the past under the direct guidance of the Holy Spirit.

"Alexander of Macedon, son of Philip, had come from the land of Kittim and defeated Darius, king of the Persians and Medes, whom he succeeded as ruler, at first of Hellas. He undertook many campaigns, gained possession of many fortresses and put the local kings to death. So he advanced to the ends of the earth, plundering nation after nation. The earth grew silent before him and his ambitious heart swelled with pride. He assembled very powerful forces and subdued provinces, nations and princes and they became his tributaries. But the time came when Alexander took to his bed in the knowledge that he was dying. He summoned his comrades, noblemen who had been brought up with him from his youth, and divided the kingdom among them while he was still alive. Alexander had reigned twelve years when he died. Each of his comrades established himself in his own region. All assumed crowns after his death, they and their heirs after them for many years, bringing increasing evils on the world. From these grew a sinful offshoot, Antiochus Epiphanes, son of King Antiochus. Once a hostage in Rome, he became king in the 137th year of the kingdom of the Greeks."

(175 B.C. The Seleucid kingdom of the Greeks dates from 312. Alexander died in 324 B.C.)

Thus begins the First Book of Maccabees. It speaks of a ruler before whom the whole world trembled and grew silent. He was very victorious. The Introductory Notes in the Jerusalem bible have this to say:

"The First Book of Maccabees places before us at the outset two irreconcilable enemies: a triumphant Hellenism with some admiring Jewish supporters; and opposed to it, the main body of the Jewish nation, faithful to the Law and the Temple. On the one hand Antiochus Epiphanes, desecrator of the Temple and persecutor; on the other, Mattathias, initiator of the crusade for religious freedom. The body of the book is divided into 3 parts, one of each of Mattathias' 3 sons, who succeeded each other as leaders of the resistance movement. The narrative covers 40 years ... Its author is a Palestinian Jew, probably writing in about 100 BC. The book is invaluable as a history of the times ... The author means to write a religious history. For him the nation's distress is a punishment for sin, and the successes of the leading figures are won by the help of God. He is a Jew, jealous for the Faith, which he perceives to be at stake in the struggle between pagan infiltration and ancestral custom. He is therefore an uncompromising foe of hellenisation and an ardent admirer of the heroes who fought for Law and Temple, winning first religious liberty and next national independence. His story tells how Judaism, the trustee of Revelation, was preserved to the world.

That the intention of the author of the Second Book is to attract and edify Judas' campaign of liberation is supported by apparitions from heaven and triumphantly concluded by divine intervention. The persecution itself is a manifestation of God's loving kindness, bringing his people to their senses before accumulating sin works final ruin ... The (Second) Book is important for its affirmation of the resurrection of the dead; sanctions in the afterlife; prayer for the dead; the spiritual fruits of martyrdom; *the intercession of the Saints.*"

The parallel with our own times and conditions is not hard to grasp, when we hear the biblical narrative continue:

"It was then that there emerged from Israel a set of renegades who led many people astray. 'Come', they said, 'let us reach an understanding with the pagans surrounding us, for since we separated ourselves from them, many misfortunes have over-taken us'. This proposal proved acceptable, and a number of the people eagerly approached the king, who authorised them to practice the pagan observances. So they built a gymnasium in Jerusalem, such as the pagans have, disguised their circumcision, and abandoned the holy Covenant, submitting to the heathen rule as willing slaves of impiety."

What orthodox Catholic is there who does *not* hear Teilhard de Chardin expressing here his disappointment with the Catholic Church in his final break with that Church in his 1929 paper *"The Human Sense"*, the origin of the natural religion which he needed for *'Building the Earth'* as the new *'Milieu Divin'* for Christ and Christianity in his evolutionary system?

The first thing the holy author teaches us here is to identify the enemy, and call him by his proper name: *enemy, renegade.* Just as Hellenism in his days was not to be considered a new, modern, inspired and exciting interpretation of the Jewish Tradition, neither is Modernism in our days a new and exciting interpretation of Catholicism. Teilhard too tried to come to an understanding with the ones left behind by Catholicism and to blame the Catholic Church both for the separation and the 'evils that have beset us since'. Anyone who cannot make up his mind about that will get devoured.

The second lesson to be learned here is the action taken by these renegades by which they can be recognised. They take pains to hide the fullness and integrity of their original loyalty: *their covenant with God*. In our days these people are ashamed of their Catholicity and want to be known as 'Christians'. They want the Marxists, the teilhardians, the scientists, and all the Protestants to know how close they are with them *in their new outlook on religion*. And since they keep on telling us *ad nauseam 'that they are the Church'*, they want to create the impression with all the outsiders that the whole Catholic Church has now adopted this new way of looking at things, and that this non-Catholic outlook has been inspired since Vatican II. And just as the author of the Second Book of Maccabees wrote for the non-Palestinian Jews, to convince them that opposition to Hellenism was God-inspired and that the embattled Jews in Palestine needed their loyal support, so it is now that many Catholics need convincing that teilhardian evolution and Modernism are evil and that opposition to them is the will of the Church.

The gruesome story of the fate that now befell the Jews is unfolded for us in graphic detail, so that we can learn step by step what will be in store for our world as a punishment for sin and apostasy, and what steps are to be taken in the light of Faith and with the discipline of the mind to overcome the evil, and once again restore on earth the full benefits of the Kingdom of God.

According to St. John in his Book of Revelation the whole world will at one time be running after the Beast; and the Beast will conquer the Saints. But he also reveals that the final victory will be given to the followers of the Lamb. In the Book of Maccabees the Holy Ghost has left us an inspired account of how that is to be done. It is but one example of many of how the Communion of Saints will inspire Catholic resourcefulness, and through it the resourcefulness of all the good Christians who wish to take part in the battle as well as in the proposed victory.

This daily contact with the Mother of God and the whole Communion of Saints provides us with the **fourth stone** in our belt: our Catholic resourcefulness with which to inspire others and to charge their drooping spirits in times of great upheavals, when everybody is running after the beast.

"Let us not lose sight of Jesus who leads us in our Faith and brings it to perfection. For the sake of the joy which was still in the future, He endured the Cross, disregarding the shamefulness of it, and from now on has taken His place at the right of God's throne. Think of the way He stood such opposition from sinners, and then you will not give up for want of courage. In the fight against sin you have not yet had to keep fighting to the point of death." (Hebr. 12:1-4)

Section V

Modernists' Meanest Mischief

"Take care that no one deceives you. Because many will come using My Name and saying: 'I am the Christ', and they will deceive many." (Mt. 24:4)

"Take care...."

That's what we have done in the previous pages, directing our first four "stones", our first four searching examinations, not at men and women, but at their deceitful doctrines and practices, *by which they are deceiving many*". Held up against Catholic Tradition, against Vatican II, against the teaching authority of the Catholic Church and against that outstanding phenomenon of our twentieth century, the Six Apparitions of Our Blessed Lady at Fatima, we wonder how any Catholic could ever be in doubt if the twisted contortions held up against the transparent Light of Catholic Faith and the pure water of Catholic doctrine could ever be taken as a substitute to satisfy the hunger of their souls. And with the ingestion of all that foreign matter, a lot of innocence has been drained away, with the result that once again the world is full of violence as it was before the Great Flood, and yes, probably even worse than it was then. For, if mankind of that ancient time, without the Redemption in the Blood of our God, without the Cross, without the Blessed Sacrament, without the Mother of God or a Church created in Her image and likeness, deserved such a massive retaliation from God, what does the world of our time deserve, which has turned its back on all these priceless gifts? What flood will be big or powerful enough to wash our world clean? The question has to be faced, even if for no other reason than for any Catholic not to be caught off guard. Which takes us back to the above quoted warning of Christ: *"Take care that no one deceives you..."*, and to our reply that in the previous four sections we *did* take care. If the warning so easily presents itself for the second time in the last section of this paper, could that be because there is still one area of deception we have overlooked? A form of mischief-making that finally would succeed in letting us be caught off guard? A pressing thought.

We have seen that those who follow false 'apparitions' and listen to their unholy 'messages' are steered by these in the wrong direction and so will be lulled into sleep to be caught off guard by their own free will. This worldwide phenomenon was dealt with in a previous section of this paper and thus cannot be meant here. There must still be another way of being caught off guard not yet dealt with. To find the answer we must look at Modernism and its innumerable adherents amongst ex-Catholics as with new eyes.

Since Pope St. Pius X has spent a whole encyclical on the heretical doctrines of these modern enemies of the Holy Church when he gave us *Pascendi* in 1907, it is hardly likely that astute Catholics are going to be caught off guard by what these enemies teach. No matter how hard they try to *"look like the Lamb"*, they only have to open their mouths and we immediately know that *"they speak like the dragon"* (Rev. 13:11). So it seems that we will have to direct our critical scrutiny away from what they teach in order to concentrate on the *praxis* of the Modernists, the way they *do* things when dealing with orthodox Catholics. To do that in an orderly fashion, we will have to make the following digression.

"Hail, full of grace, the Lord is with thee; blessed art thou amongst women". (Lk. 1:28)

"And Elizabeth was filled with the Holy Ghost. She cried out in a loud voice: 'Blessed art thou among women, and blessed is the Fruit of thy womb.... And blessed art thou for believing that the promise made to thee by the Lord would be fulfilled'." (Lk. 1:41,45)

"As for those people who were once brought into the Light, and tasted the gift from heaven, and received a share from the Holy Spirit, and appreciated the good message of God and the powers of the world to come, and yet in spite of this have fallen away: – it is impossible for them to be renewed a second time. They cannot be repentant if they have willfully crucified the Son of God and openly mocked Him." (Hebr. 6:4-6)

"Is there any need to say anymore? There is no time for me to give an account of Gideon, Barak, Samson, Jephthah, or of David, Samuel and the prophets. These were men who through Faith conquered kingdoms, did what is right and earned the promises. They stopped the mouths of lions; put out blazing fires, and emerged unscathed from battle. They were weak people who were given strength to be brave in war and drive back foreign invaders. Some came back to their wives as from the dead, but others submitted to torture, refusing release so that they would rise again to a better life. Some had to bear being pilloried and flogged, or even chained up in prison. They were stoned, or sawn in half, or beheaded; they were homeless, and dressed in the skins of sheep and goats. They were penniless, and were given nothing but ill-treatment. They were too good for this world and they went out to live in deserts and mountains and in caves and ravines. These are all heroes of Faith but they did not receive what was promised, since God had made provision for us to have something better, and they were not to reach perfection except with us. With so many witnesses as a great cloud on every side of us, we too then should throw off everything that hinders us...." (Hebr. 11:32-12:1)

"If the soul has its own embodiment, so does the spirit have its own embodiment. As Scripture says: the first man, Adam, *became a living soul* (Gen. 2:7), but the last Adam has become a life-giving spirit." (1 Cor. 15:44-45)

"I praise You for I am wonderfully made.
O Lord, You search me and You know me,
You know my resting and my rising,
You discern my purpose from afar;
You mark when I walk or lie down,
All my ways lie open to You.
For it was You who created my being,
Knit me together in my mother's womb.
I thank you for the wonder of my being,
For the wonders of all your creation.
Already You know my soul,
My body held no secret from You
When I was being fashioned in secret
And moulded in the depths of the earth." (Ps. 138)

These texts taken from sacred Scripture prove beyond *any* doubt that every man, woman and child is **unique**. That each human being is first of all a living *soul* to be able to live the corruptible life on this earth. But these texts also show that we can receive the *spirit* to live already here on earth the incorruptible Life of Faith. We must now conclude this digression with a few well-chosen texts to see what this means. But before this is done I want to put stress on what St. Paul says in the second last quote above: The *soul* has its **own** embodiment. The unique soul of every man, woman and child has its own embodiment: a unique *body* by which that unique soul is recognised as is so eloquently expressed by the Psalmist: *"You knit me together in my mother's womb"* And the unique share of each man, woman and child in the Holy Spirit, this *spirit* in man also has its own embodiment: the way the Faith (Jewish, Christian, Catholic) is being lived. People who do *not* enjoy a share in the Supernatural Life while here on earth only have a *soul* according to St. Paul which will help them to live here on earth but will not be enough to get them to heaven, as the above quotes from the Letter to the Hebrews so clearly show. St. Paul calls all those witnesses *"the heroes of Faith"*.

This uniqueness of every human being is inalienable. This means that the responsibility for our own actions cannot be transferred to somebody else. After the Fall of our first parents Adam tried to pass the blame for **his** action onto Eve, and Eve tried to pass the blame for **her** action onto the devil. But God would not have a bar of that, and – as Scripture testifies – it is still the same for us.

"We shall all have to stand before the Judgement Seat of God, as Scripture says: 'By My life – it is the Lord who speaks – every knee shall bend before Me and every tongue shall praise God. It is to God, therefore, that each of us must give an account of himself'." (Rom.14:12)

"Let each of you examine his own conduct; if you find anything to boast about, it will at least be something of your own, not just something better than your neighbour has. Everyone has his own burden to carry." (Gal.6:4-5)

"For all the truth about us will be brought out in the law court of Christ and each of us will get what he deserves for the things he did in the body, good or bad." (2 Cor. 5:10)

If God has intimate knowledge *'of how we are knitted together'*, and *'of our resting and rising'*, as well as *'of our purpose'*, then He is also fully aware *'of all the truth about us'*. This may be a scary thought if we think we are alone. Therefore, in anticipation of coming to grips with one of Modernism's meanest deceptions (to which all the above quotes prepare us), we had better finish with a couple of reassuring quotes, one from the Old Testament and its parallel in the New.

"The Lord God says this: 'I am going to look after My flock Myself and keep all of it in view. As a shepherd keeps all his flock in view when he stands up in the middle of his scattered sheep, so shall I keep My sheep in view. I shall rescue them from wherever they have been scattered during the mist and darkness ... I shall look for the lost one, bring back the stray, bandage the wounded and make the weak strong. I shall watch over the fat and healthy. I shall be a true shepherd to them'." (Ez. 34:11-16)

"Jesus spoke this parable to the scribes and Pharisees:

'What man among you with a hundred sheep, losing one, would not leave the ninety-nine in the wilderness and go after the missing one till he found it? And when he found it, would he not joyfully take it on his shoulders, and then, when he got home, call together his friends and neighbours? "Rejoice with me", he would say, "I have found my sheep that was lost". In the same way, I tell you, there will be more rejoicing in heaven over one repentant sinner than over ninety-nine virtuous men who have no need of repentance'." (Lk. 15:3-7)

Now that we have been suitably prepared from the best possible source there is to understand what comes next, we may start asking ourselves 'What have all these quotes from Sacred Scripture in common?' 'What does God's Revelation reveal in the inerrant Word of God, the Bible?' 'What do we find out no matter where we open any book of the Old or the New Testament?'

- We read about *individuals* who are uniquely created by God. And we find out that each individual soul created by God has been given by God a unique task and a unique *purpose* to be taken care of in *this* life here on earth.
- And that consequently, each of these created souls can only do their own thing, and are all responsible for their own actions in their own circumstances.

First, there is the Blessed Virgin Mary, the one who, as a pure creature (so as not to compare Her to Her Son) did more for man-

kind in her own person than all the other human beings put together.

Then there is Elizabeth, John the Baptist, St. Paul himself and
that whole *'cloud of witnesses'* those men and women of Faith he
calls up before the Bar of History: Abel, Enoch, Noah, Abraham,
Isaac, Jacob, Sarah, Joseph, Moses, Rahab the prostitute, and con-
fessing to have no time to go on to mention the deeds brought
about by the Faith of Gideon, Barak, Samson, Jephthah, David,
Samuel and the Prophets. Add to that all the Saints we know who
ever lived in the New Testament, those shining examples beckon-
ing us to come to their homeland, and to forget all the glamour and
corruptible things this earth has to offer.

And what have we got? What does all this add up to?

It adds up to this, that, as St. Paul testifies, anything great for
God and mankind, anything beneficial, powerful and lasting was
brought about by **individuals**, by men and women of Faith.

*And the one great fact that has emerged in the second half of our
20th century is:* **that Modernists intensely dislike individuals
enough to ruin this picture....**

Why would that be so?

Because human beings who exert their individualism, and especially those with a deep Catholic Faith, express their belief that,
having been created in the image and likeness of God, they are first
and foremost themselves, having received from God their own
uniqueness and their own purpose. *This makes them unmanagea-
ble for Modernist bullies.* For human individuals are more than individuals: they are **persons**, and it is in their personhood that they
resemble God.

So what then is a person?

A person (and this could never be expressed any better, because it comes from the great St. Thomas Aquinas) is the **owner** of his or her acts, and this ownership, as all the above quotes from Sacred Scripture testify, cannot be delegated, transferred, minimised or abandoned. It remains the person's property. And it is for this inalienable property, this divine right, in which human beings resemble the *three Divine Persons,* <u>that all Modernists have a great dislike for all those Catholic individuals</u> who see through their hypocrisy and falsehoods and stand up to them.

This brings us to the core of their *meanest mischief* by which they vent their intense dislike and fight off these Catholic individuals.

All those who, through their true Faith and their love of God, live in state of grace, form a very mysterious bond called *the Communion of Saints.* This bond, being an Article of Faith, has been revealed by God and so comes from God. It is composed of *individuals* as, according to the above quotes, God only recognises individuals and persons. Now if Modernists already experience great difficulty controlling Catholic individuals, especially persons of Faith, that is, those who really take possession of their good acts and exert their ownership, then they have no hope of exerting their bullying tactics over the Communion of Saints.

And it was their intense dislike for *the Communion of Saints* that finally gave them the idea of how to fight those Catholics who are at home in it. For it was for this reason: for the destruction of the individual Catholic person and for the destruction of the influence the Communion of Saints has over those Catholics, that the

Modernists latched onto something that does not exist, and to which they gave a name that has no meaning: *'community'*.

Allow me to explain.

Those who consciously live in the *Communion of Saints* know exactly what this Communion hopes for, and believes in, and loves. They know its goodness and Truth, and its unity, that which binds together the Saints in Heaven, the souls in Purgatory and those in state of grace on earth. They feel at home in it as in the *City of God*. For they know that they are no strangers in that City; they know how well-known they are themselves and how appreciated they are as individuals, as lies so eloquently expressed in *all* the quotes above. They are in daily contact with the Saints to be inspired by them in their love for God, Church and neighbour.

And they know who do *not* belong to this Communion, those who are attached to their sins, the women on the pill, those who live in irregular relationships, the murderers, abortionists, thieves, pedophiles, and all the other outsiders who all shelter in *'the community'* but are *not* found in the *Communion of Saints*.

On the other hand, what does *'the community'* think? No one knows and no one cares. What does it want? No one knows what it wants. What does it believe in? What binds it together? No one knows. It is just an agglomerate of people each with their own private thoughts, fears, plans and sins. *'The community'* harbours a lot of sinners who would never be part of the Communion of Saints. There is no cohesion or unity in *the community*, nothing that sets it apart, nothing that guides or inspires it. The mere fact that some people live in the same area has never created a bond, except maybe in times when there is a common threat. But when left to their own devices, each 'member' follows his own private thoughts and pursues his own private plans which can be as contrary as any other member's plans and thoughts are. And these are hidden under a veneer of some frivolous camaraderie to hide the fact that he or she never really feels part of a *'community'* except maybe when driven by some politician or *a minister of religion.*

Now all this may be quite understandable that people cannot come to grips with what is so ill-defined as *'the community',* where every contrary thought lives and finds a home, were it not for the *praxis* of the Modernists we talked about before, the *use* they make of this concept *community* when dealing with orthodox Catholics. With Catholics that is, who refuse to be bullied by them, considering themselves as belonging to the Communion of Saints *where everything is well-defined.* The very fact that such Catholics live out in their lives Christ's commandment to love God first and their neighbour as themselves, and thus in their quiet way are far more charitable, out-going and Christ-like than any 'member' of a fictitious *'community',* is the very fact that makes them so loathed by Modernist priests. For such Catholics show that, as individuals and as persons, they are in charge of their own Catholic actions, and so maintain a Catholic identity that is totally opposed to the 'catholicity' that emanates from Modernism and is enforced by Modernist priests and their 'catholic' community stooges. And all of a sudden this hideous concept of 'community' has become the **recycling bin** into which all these free and easy children of God, Catholics who are the owners of their own actions and stand up for the Catholic Church, must be thrown in order that they can be controlled by

their Modernist bullies and come out as twisted as they are themselves.

Thus the references to 'community' are never-ending as if coming from a cracked long-playing record. And Hell has no mercy!
These Catholics are subjected to all sorts of sometimes subtle,
sometimes brutal and public humiliations and persecutions, even
by priests who pride themselves as being 'on their side'.

Loud singing of songs which no longer represent their Catholic
Faith, but are composed by Modernists who, like John Wesley,
have seen the power of singing to promote the new twists in Catholic thinking. Abuses in the Liturgy of the Mass, piped music and
tape recorders, soloists, announcements, jokes, laughter, clapping,
talking and all the other din that makes the House of God resemble
a cinema.

And on top of that there is another reason why *community* is
such a handy instrument in the hands of Modernism. Modernist
priests are no good shepherds. They loathe 'to stand in the middle
of their flock' and keep all of it in view. *And they most certainly do
not want to go after the lost sheep,* being lost themselves. Nor do
they care 'for the fat and healthy ones'. In other words, they have
put a barrier between themselves and the really Catholic part of
their flock. One can hear them talking and laughing outside after
Mass with a lot of banter and hilarity, but only about trivial things.
The things that matter or are a worry to orthodox Catholics are
never allowed to be brought up. To priests like that there are no
problems. Is it not true that nowadays in nearly every parish the
majority of parishioners consists of 'catholics' who love the freedom of conscience that Modernism brought with it, a freedom they

never enjoyed in the Communion of Saints. Such parishioners are quite happy to be fully paid-up members of the modern salvation club: *the parish community,* in which 'salvation' is inevitable. So, after Sunday Mass, the *parish community* together with the PP slips back into the wider outside community, while the orthodox Catholics lose contact with the PP and are locked up in some imaginary paddock to be safely stored away out of sight, <u>so as not to upset the parish community</u>. For all he cares they can look after themselves until the next Sunday, when they are temporarily released in order that the whole tragedy can start all over again. And so the suffering goes on, year in, year out, with hardly any relief in sight.

And of course here we recognise the danger we talked about on the first page of this final section: the danger of being 'sucked in', *the real possibility of being caught off guard.* If the *majority* of parishioners in any parish consists nowadays of 'catholics' who have gone over to the new religion, then this shows that the pressure to *conform,* to leave the Communion of Saints and join a non-existing 'parish community' was too great for these original Catholics, and thus must not be underestimated to be strong enough to seduce others. If a PP sees that the majority of his parishioners do not mind joining in with modernistic songs, have no objections to loud, piped music, abuses in the Liturgy, or laughter, clapping and talking in church, why should he think they are lost? They only follow his example and he does not consider himself lost! After all, has he not made sure that they are being taken care of by the *'parish community'*? <u>All the other Catholics have to do is join in</u>. Thus, in the fictitious absence of any lost sheep, he has freed himself to ignore the real Catholics of his flock, to spend happy hours with his *parish community,* attend seminars and lectures, or to read questionable books which will further erode his already dwindling spiritual immune system.

Meanwhile of course, our dear Catholic friends, far from being buried in the *parish community* or being locked up in some paddock, use their God-given natural understanding and the supernatural insights of their Catholic Faith to undo the evil of Modernism in their sphere of influence. They prove to be irrepressible.

They do their own thing in the sight of God because, as real natural and supernaturally ordered *persons* they are the only and inalienable *owners* of their own actions for the spread of the Kingdom of God here on earth, as millions of God's children have done before them and will continue to do so after them. Under no circumstances will they ever allow a *parish community* or anybody else to take charge over what is their God-given right and obligation.

And with this we have uncovered the last of our 'five smooth stones'.

It is our firm resistance against any attempts by one of the gravest misdeeds of our Modernist adversaries: *the destruction of our Catholic individuality* by making us leave the Communion of Saints in order to make us enter the vestibule of the 'Church of Darkness': a non-existing 'community' where everything goes, even the most contrary things....

This **fifth stone** too, as were the previous four, is not directed against flesh and blood, but against yet another insidious, looming shape that surrounds us everywhere we go and is directly threatening us and our children. And we may be forgiven for directing our readers' attention once again to what has already appeared in this book as the best summing up for the form this holy resistance may take. I am referring to what was stressed and held up at Fatima in 1917. In the hands of intrepid Catholics this is bound to destroy Modernism and the insidious use it makes of 'community' to make Catholic individuality and the Communion of Saints inoperable.

For that it deserves no mercy.....

"It is not those who say to Me 'Lord, Lord,' who will enter the Kingdom of Heaven, but the person(!) who does the will of My Father in Heaven. When the Day comes many will say to Me, 'Lord, Lord, did we not prophesy (preach) **in Your Name, cast out demons** (baptise) **in Your Name, work many miracles** (change bread and wine into Your Body and Blood) **in Your Name?' Then I shall tell them to their faces: I have never known you: away from Me you evil men!"** (Matt. 7:21-23)

From this we learn that what Modernist priests do is very serious in the eyes of Him who founded His Catholic Church on the Rock of St. Peter, not for the destruction of Catholic Faith and Catholic individuality, but for making them shine in all their glory.

Please pray for these priests! It is very telling that Our Blessed Lord uses the word *"many"* in the above quote.

Epilogue

But then, when our adversaries at last begin to realize that we have become the weakness of God, *"which is still stronger than human strength"* (1 Cor. 1:25), what then? When it starts to sink in that our five smooth stones were not directed at them but at their doctrines and practices? At the powers in the air, their masters and slave drivers? When they start to understand that after all we have become as vulnerable as the Lamb of God was in His days, then what? *When they realize that they can put a belt around us and drag us where we would rather not go,* (John 21:18) what then? Then we will have to be prepared, for then their scorn and their hatred will know no bounds.

At what were the five wounds of Our Blessed Lord directed? Certainly at the defeat of the powers in the air, the power of *the* enemy who held all of us captive since Adam's fall. But after that, what was their target? And it is there that our enemies are going to make their greatest mistake, the same mistake as was made by the Jewish Sanhedrin and the Roman soldiers. For Our Lord's and our own wounds are not aimed at any *thing*. Not aimed at anything else but themselves! This time *they themselves* are the target This irresistible power sprung from the wound in His Sacred Heart, the source of His infinite Mercy. *"Father, forgive them for they do not know what they are doing"*.

Then they will release what we briefly talked about on the first page of this final section, that second Great Flood meant to wash the whole world clean from its terrible sins: the persecutions under Antichrist. And by that Flood many will be saved.

For that we need *training* and preparation, and great love for our enemies.

For that we need *individuals* who are prepared to stand apart from the crowd.

For that we need *persons* who fully own their own actions.....

And remember this.

The storm-tossed boat in which the Son of Man was lying asleep needed to have had on board only **one individual** to tell the other disciples: *"Leave the Master asleep. Awake or asleep, He is powerful enough to save us from death by drowning"*. And not only would they have obeyed him, but, while asleep, the good Lord would have calmed the storm at the display of such a Faith in Him.

Appendix

Miracle of the Sun: Astronomer's Verdict

(Appendix added by the Editor)

In the nineteen forties an Italian Jesuit scientist, Fr. Pio Scatizzi, undertook an exhaustive study of the solar miracle. He was professor of algebra and trigonometry at the Gregorian University in Rome. Fr Scatizzi was an outstanding mathematician and astronomer, highly esteemed in the Italian scientific world.

A Critical Note
By Pio Scatizzi, S.J.

In world history, outside ordinary eclipses, nothing prodigious has been recorded of the sun, with the single exception of the biblical miracle of Joshua-the day's standstill of sun and moon. This fact and no other marks Fatima with a stupendous singularity quite apart from the rest of the story.

The thousands of pilgrims, as we know, were caught in pouring rain, while gusts of wind swept the rocky hillsides. Suddenly, at midday, the heavens opened and the clouds drew back to the horizon, leaving the air pure and clear as a mirror. Such would be the case after prolonged and copious rain, when the air becomes more transparent than usual and appears to have been washed. At this moment the sun begins to pale, and it may be argued that the diminution of light could have been caused by mist or flakes of mist suspended in the air. After all those hours of rain and all that hu-

234 Select Works of Frits Albers, Vol. 2

midity, it would be logical to suspect that at least some fragments of mist would remain in the atmosphere. At first sight such doubts might be justified, since many witnesses describe the sun's disc as being opaque, silvered, or like mother-of-pearl.

Yet we can admit without hesitation that the sun looked opaque, with a well-defined rim, and at the same time prove that there was no intervening mist. In fact, we can postulate this alternative: either the mist was light or it was dense. I define a "light" mist that which exists between zero and the extreme point at which the eye cannot, with impunity, be fixed on the sun. I call a "dense" mist that which exists from this point until there is complete occultation. Now it is certain that the first alternative must be excluded, for the sun appeared like mother-of-pearl on which the vision could easily be fixed. There remains, therefore, the second alternative. But if the mist were dense, the sun's disc would not have been clearly defined. For, in fact, when a dense, damp fog veils it, there is formed in the surrounding atmosphere a kind of aureole or crown (not in the technical and astronomical sense of the word) which, so to speak, confirms the presence of mist. Yet all affirm that the sky behind the sun was perfectly clear. Now between this and a mist capable of dominating solar light, there would seem to be an excessive difference, one may say a contradiction: the sky a clean background and at the same time a mist obscuring the sun.

This opaqueness of the sun in a clear sky was but the beginning of events, for immediately there began to radiate from its center, thousands upon thousands of colored monochromatic lights in sectors, which, in the form of spirals, began to whirl around the center of the solar disc in such a manner that the sun itself seemed to turn on itself rather like a catherine wheel, while the colored rays spread out in a centrifugal movement covering the sky as far as the curtain of clouds, and turning everything various colors as if by magic. Such a spectacle of red, yellow, green and violet rays from the sun, spreading and sweeping over the sky, cannot be explained by any known laws, nor has such a thing been seen before.

Could it have been a rainbow? Obviously not, for the simple reason that a rainbow is usually stationary. Further, the rainbow is drawn on a vertical plane opposite the sun and does not originate in the solar disc itself, but in the opposite line of vision. The eye rests on the summit of a cone on whose base rests the plane of the arch. The solar rays, which are parallel and horizontal, radiate form behind the observer, not from the front, and with a penetrating action reflect themselves once or twice in the falling drops of water, returning to the eye with the dispersion of the iris. In the case under review, on the contrary, the phenomenon is one of radiation over the whole circle of the horizon with uniform and continuous movement. Certainly there can occur other prismatic effects in the atmosphere, but they are seen, as is well known, at dawn or sunset. The air then operates as a prism, dispersing the light in various colored beams-those of the spectrum.

In the case of Fatima, it is extremely difficult to place such a phenomenon within a framework when outside the solar disc there was only limpid air without any reflecting agent, as with a rainbow, when along each monochromatic ray numberless drops of water renew the prismatic effect. In Fatima, as seen by motionless observers, the monochromatic sectors appeared to revolve and to subsist without any support. We must conclude that each colored ray was maintained autonomously, with its origin in the solar body, the air providing no means to transmission. At an altitude of 42 degrees 44'- that of the sun at midday in October-clear air, in some measure disturbed by wind, could not of itself cause a phenomenon of spectral dispersion of autonomous rotating rays.

The only comparable phenomenon is, perhaps, the aurora borealis. Professor Vercelli, in his book, "The Air", quotes a description by Mr. Herdel of an exceptional aurora which was seen in the state of Iowa on the night of May 14, 1921. Taking this account as a base for comparison, I note a great divergence between the two events. In Fatima, stable, compact, above all homogeneous. The aurora was variable, disordered, unstable. Further, it is proved that the zone of maximum occurrence of the aurora borealis is limited by a quasi-parallel running through North Cape-Northern Siberia-coast of Alaska-Hudson Bay-Labrador-Iceland and back to North Cape in Norway. We can then be nearly certain that on the 50th parallel the aurora cannot be seen-at least according to current theory.

The aurora borealis is caused by trajectories of electrons, or better, according to Vegard, by particles thrown off by the sun and diverted to the magnetic field of the earth. Then, coming in contact with the air, they give origin to the variegated lights which can be observed. The quasi-parallel trajectories which pass through the magnetic north are seen by us converging and diverging only by an effect of perspective. In substance, the aurora borealis are inherent in the terrestrial magnetic poles and thence to the "hyper-boreal" regions-hence their name.

In spite of all this, one cannot absolutely excluded the possibility of the aurora borealis being seen in low latitudes. In fact one was observed in Rome in 1938, but one fact alone distinguishes the Fatima phenomenon from this and other appearances of the aurora. The origin of the lights in Fatima was in the sun, from whence they sprang, whereas during the true aurora the sun is always invisible. Apart from this, the latitude of Fatima (39 degrees 36') is even lower than that of Rome. Also the synchronizing, revolving movement of the sectors and their three stops at regular intervals (according to witnesses) is far from the irregular, disordered movements, the disappearance and reappearance of light as described in Mr. Herdel's account. Lastly, if there had been a true aurora borealis it would have been observed in some European observatory.

It now remains to examine the third phase of the phenomenon, that is to say the movement of the sun, which appeared to detach itself from the sky and to fall on the earth in a zigzag path. It can be affirmed that such a phenomenon is outside and against all natural and astronomical laws. It appears that with this final occurrence, all doubts as to the natural origin of the events, all skepticism on our part, must be laid aside.

At this point it would be well to refresh our motives for belief in such an unheard of incident. The number and nature of the witnesses exceed all requirements for verification. With twelve such, the law justifies the execution of a man. In this case, eyewitnesses numbered some 70,000.

To resume our study: first, we have the rotation of the sun and the various colors; secondly, a movement outside the normal daily path of the sun in the heavens. In the first case there would be a normal admiration such as would be excited by a first view of an aurora borealis. There would be no cause for terror. Yet, suddenly, without the intervention of any new factor, the multitude is seized with terror as if menaced by a cataclysm. Everyone feels threatened by imminent catastrophe. There is a sensation that the sun is about to fall on the earth; that it is being torn from the cosmic laws of its eternal path. Hence the invocations, the prayers, the cries of affliction, as in a universal cataclysm.

Observe well the second phase. It is not religious hysteria, nor a species of pentecostal fervor. It is sheer panic in the presence of Him who alone can dominate the forces of the universe. Contemporary accounts will show that it was not a case of suggestion, but that an objective vision was the cause of the panic which, when it had passed, left everyone perfectly calm, contented even, at having witnessed a prodigy which had been exactly foretold and anxiously awaited. How also could everyone have seen the danger pass at one and the same moment?

Of the historical reality of this event there can be no doubt whatever. That it was outside and against known laws can be proved by certain simple scientific considerations.

The "movement" of the sun is relative to the earth's own. The orbit of the latter is nearly an ellipse of extremely small excentricity. The daily transitional movement of the earth-even with its velocity of 18 miles a second-is projectively imperceptible. Much less would it be so during the ten minutes' duration of the phenomenae: ten minutes are sufficient, as was the case in Fatima, for a generic qualitative observation, they would not suffice for the observation with the naked eye of a solar dislocation which can be known only in relation to the distances of the zodiac constellations.

Conclusion: The above-mentioned solar phenomena were not noted in any observatory. Impossible that they should escape the notice of so many astronomers and indeed the other inhabitants of the hemisphere. It must then be admitted that there is no question of an astronomical or meteorological phenomenon as we have already said. We are thus confronted with an inescapable dilemma. Either all the observers in Fatima were collectively deceived and erred in their testimony, or we must suppose an extra-natural intervention. Given the indubitable reference to God, and the general context of the story, it seems that we must attribute to Him alone the most obvious and colossal miracle of history.

www.ingramcontent.com/pod-product-compliance
Lightning Source LLC
Chambersburg PA
CBHW070026100426
42740CB00013B/2608